Why Church?

CHRISTIANITY AS IT WAS MEANT TO BE

SCOTT COWDELL

Foreword by Ian S. Markham

Church
PUBLISHING

Unless otherwise noted, the Scripture quotations are from New Revised Standard Version Bible, copyright © 1989 National Council of the Churches of Christ in the United States of America. Used by permission. All rights reserved worldwide.

Church Publishing
19 East 34th Street
New York, NY 10016
www.churchpublishing.org

Cover image by Master of the Housebook, The Last Supper, 1475–80, courtesy the National Museums of Berlin, Picture Gallery / Christoph Schmidt
Cover design by Newgen
Typeset by Nord Compo

ISBN 978-1-64065-736-6 (paperback)
ISBN 978-1-64065-737-3 (eBook)

Library of Congress Control Number: 2024935990

Dedicated with gratitude
to the Dean, faculty, and students of the
Virginia Theological Seminary
of the Episcopal Church
from their Winter–Spring 2023 Dean's Scholar

"High and beautiful is his holy hill:
it is the joy of all the earth."

Psalm 48:2

Also by Scott Cowdell

Rejoice and Be Glad: Gospel Preaching for Christian Festivals

Mimetic Theory and its Shadow: Girard, Milbank, and Ontological Violence

Church Matters: Essays and Addresses on Ecclesial Belonging

René Girard and the Nonviolent God

René Girard and Secular Modernity: Christ, Culture, and Crisis

Abiding Faith: Christianity Beyond Certainty, Anxiety, and Violence

The Ten Commandments and Ethics Today

God's Next Big Thing: Discovering the Future Church

A God for This World

Is Jesus Unique? A Study of Recent Christology

Atheist Priest? Don Cupitt and Christianity

Contents

Foreword

Why Church? The question is so simple, yet so complicated. For those of us who fall under that generic heading "western Christianity", we are all alert to the challenges of Church. Skepticism has made faith implausible; the breakdown in voluntary associations has made joining problematic; and advocates for church are drowned out by voices advocating for a cafeteria spirituality, where you can pick and choose the items that you find most attractive.

There has been an explosion of articles and books that agonize over the question "why church". The most serious come from proponents of congregational studies who document with care the decline in participation, the challenging of passing the faith from generation to generation, and the breakdown in religious habits among the young. These studies leave you despairing. Others offer "try this" tips. The precise initiative changes over time. Sometimes it is contemporary praise music with a band rather than hymns accompanied by an organ. Others argue for the church to be the hub of the community and focus on social activism and advocacy for those around them. Others call for a resolute return to the faith that was, where we resist the call to include those who are LGBTQ plus. Others call for the opposite—a church that includes everyone. Others again argue for a more effective accommodation of contemporary skepticism and then suggest a faith that is little more than deism in modern attire. Then we have the cyber options: an avatar church, church online, and the YouTube church in your pajamas. If you live long enough in this literature, then you are left with a deep awareness of the crisis of the moment. The problem we have is that the critique facing the church is deeply serious and threatening to our survival and many of the proposed solutions do not start to understand (and therefore know how to confront) that critique.

Scott Cowdell has provided a study that both understands the challenges and sees the way forward. The way forward is surprisingly traditional: to recover a sense of Christian hospitality through the Eucharist. His critique is informed. Charles Taylor figures prominently; he understands the energy of churches in the global south; and he knows the skeptical mindset. He is a very effective tour guide: he knows the literature extremely well, and he is gentle with his interlocuters. In proposing a way forward, Scott Cowdell is acutely aware of the challenges that his vision faces. He grapples in detail with the "spiritual but not religious" mood of our time. He acknowledges that a Eucharistic approach cannot be synonymous with church being prejudiced or boring. But this remains the way forward because it is the Eucharist that tells the story of the faith that Christians inhabit. And if Christianity is to continue, then it will only be recognizable in the future provided we continue to inhabit this story through the Eucharist.

To be the right person at the right time to write the right book is a rare combination. However, in this book the combination is being realized. Scott Cowdell is the right person. He comes to the questions around ecclesiology as a theologian who has written on Christology, philosophical theology, and René Girard; he is a theologian who knows both the parish and theological education intimately. It is the right time because we are living at a time when the tired debates around secularization and church growth desperately need new strands of theological reflection and analysis. The result is that this is the "right" book; it has the potential to reorientate our thinking and understanding.

It is a gift to write a book with real learning in such a way that it could be used as a Lent study book. Scott Cowdell has this gift. Every sentence is carefully framed and measured;

there is a significant literature supporting every assertion. Yet every reader can grasp the point, see the significance, and grow because of the encounter.

There have been moments when a book spoke to a particular historic moment. Often these books argue for a radical understanding of the faith: John Robinson's *Honest to God* or John Shelby Spong's *Why Christianity Must Change or Die* are two illustrations. Scott Cowdell's *Why Church?* has the potential to speak to our moment. But instead of taking us away from the faith, this text can bring us closer to the God revealed in our Lord Jesus Christ.

The Very Rev. Ian S. Markham, Ph.D.
Dean and President of Virginia Theological Seminary;
President of The General Theological Seminary, New York;
Professor of Theology and Ethics

Acknowledgments

I thank Dean Ian Markham for his invitation to come as Dean's Scholar to Virginia Theological Seminary (VTS)—outside Washington in Alexandria, Virginia—and for the gracious hospitality that he and Lesley showed us. It was an honor to be at VTS in the bicentennial year of this largest and best-resourced seminary in the Anglican Communion, which generations of residents have referred to as the Holy Hill. Our nine weeks there—sharing meals and conviviality in the Dining Hall, with worship at Immanuel Chapel—were memorable and productive. Ian has also graciously provided a Foreword. Many thanks, too, to Dr Mitzi Budde and her staff at the Bishop Payne Library for a congenial place to work, the warmest of welcomes, and every assistance. During that time, I was able to pull together and write Chapters 3–6.

I greatly appreciated the responses and feedback from friends and colleagues near and far who subsequently read the manuscript for me: Anthony Bartlett, Greg Burke OCD, Chris Fleming, Chris Lewis, Alison Milbank, and +Stephen Pickard.

I am indebted to Airié Stuart and all at Church Publishing in New York, especially Justin Hoffman, Mark Powers, and Anne Zaccardelli. Also to Christopher Brennan, way down in Tasmania, for one more indexing job. Once again, I thank my wife, Lisa Carley, who has been a welcome sounding board and a solid support during one more writing project. Not only that, but she leavened our stay at VTS by learning to play the ukulele!

Introduction

A highlight of my role as honorary associate priest in our local Anglican parish was the opportunity to spend time with the youth group. I was invited along because some parents thought that their teenagers might like a theologian—supposedly, an expert on the ins and outs of Christian belief—to give a talk and then answer questions. To my surprise, it kicked off well and I was asked back several times. Following an initial talk about ethics, we then explored different aspects of creation belief according to the book of Genesis, after which a few more sessions were devoted to various of Jesus's Zen-like parables in the Gospels.

But then I began to wonder why all the intelligent enthusiasm of these impressive and likeable young people did not reliably carry over to Sunday morning. I would look down from the pulpit or the altar and see few if any of their faces, even if their parents were present. They were often energized by the ideas we discussed at youth group, and the breakthrough for humanity that Jesus brought. They seemed to appreciate the silent meditation that we practiced at the beginning of each session. But the Sunday Eucharist in that family-sized congregation, with people who loved them and had known some of them all their lives, was a different matter. They could think the thoughts and value the insights, and even own the Christian faith to some extent, though without much sense of attraction let alone obligation toward the Church and its Eucharist. And this despite specific promises made at their Confirmation. Why?

Pondering this led me to think about pulling together a short book about the Church to cast light on this quandary. Because I am not alone in my concerns. What I encountered in my small corner of things is in fact the major crisis of mainstream Western churches in microcosm. Clergy and lay leaders everywhere struggle to reconnect with lost generations and demographics, often with an inadequate sense of what to do or where to start.

A related scenario arises in the sort of pastoral relationship that I occasionally stumble into with a spiritual seeker from wholly outside the Christian faith. These are the people often described as spiritual but not religious. Over time in such conversations, I try to listen carefully and patiently, I bend over backward to draw spiritual insights from scripture and Church tradition, I make connections between doctrine and experience, and I try to show that faith is a friend rather than an enemy of reason, science, and human freedom, all the while holding up Jesus Christ whom I love as key to discovering both God and the meaning of our lives. I can connect the Church to feminism, postmodernism, and postcolonial thought, and no doubt this helps. But as a theologian from a high-Church liturgical tradition, where my own heart and mind found their lifetime's alignment, I want to lead the spiritual seeker further. I want them to "come and see" where Christ lives and loves, in the fellowship of word and sacrament, among the gathered people who are being slowly converted into his likeness.

But you know what could well happen. This further stage is often a bridge too far—indeed, one could think, almost invariably so. I want to say that rising with the swell of God's love apart from the Church is like trying to surf a big wave without a surfboard. Discovering this eternal love is meant to happen where that love is historically grounded. But send that spiritual seeker along to church, or bring them along with you, and what might the result be? Those who try this with spiritual seekers may well find that the connection fails to spark, perhaps as a result of entrenched preconceptions—or worse, that an encounter with the Church has raised concerns even for an open-minded inquirer.

Whether or not the Church proves off-putting in those circumstances, there are cultural barriers standing between the modern Western imagination and Church involvement. So, for instance, today's typical romantic temperament cannot begin to imagine it, nor can today's widespread therapeutic mindset find any place for it. There are much more interesting avenues for individuals to pursue if life is about the search for intensity, satisfaction, and personal connection. Church would not even register by comparison. Besides, everyone knows that Christian life makes demands on our relationships and priorities. Such long-form, typically low-key resolve is too unfashionably serious, too un-cool, too totally inconceivable for many. Today's spiritual imagination is regularly affronted by Christianity's traditional disciplines and exclusive claims. So, spirituality, even faith—yes! But Church; but Eucharist? What? No!

One final scenario pertains to the gathered Church itself. Many regular worshippers in mainline liturgical churches lack conviction about their involvement, content with habit where one might hope for habit with conviction. In traditions where the creed is recited in worship, they may be prepared to join in saying that "We believe in one, holy, catholic and apostolic Church" though without registering the claim on their loyalty that this credal article implies. One could also wonder whether the earlier credal articles are being recited with any greater conviction (i.e., the ones about God the Father, Jesus Christ as Lord, and the Holy Spirit). Indeed, I know Anglicans who resent the creed, some of whom stand silently in the liturgy while others around them are reciting it—they find it unbelievable, or irrelevant to what they see themselves doing, or else as imposing unwelcome cognitive content when they are primarily at church for the atmosphere and the music. This is not a condemnation, but merely the sober recognition of what does and does not bring people to church and keep them there. A sense of recollection, peacefulness, or even transcendence might still be found, or else some moral obligation might be summoned up, or God's protection and providence might be gratefully acknowledged—a major aspect of simple religious faith, both ancient and modern—but for many their presence in the liturgy is not perceived as a lifegiving encounter with Christ. Indeed, six Cs have helped to sustain a lot of churchgoing: culture, class, consolation, continuity, community, and conspicuousness (i.e., being seen, including being seen to be a certain sort of person).

Pastoral experience teaches that Christian belief for a proportion of churchgoers in mainstream liturgical churches is largely unexamined, tenuous, tinged with a more-or-less embarrassed skepticism, and prone to ready collapse. An unfortunate pastoral encounter, an unwelcome challenge to firmly-held opinion from the pulpit, an upset to faith in God's providence through some unfavorable circumstance, a disruption to churchgoing habits—caused by moving to a new locality, perhaps, or in recent years by the suspension of public worship during long COVID lockdowns—can see Church involvement abandoned. Sometimes the arrival of an unsympathetic or irritating new priest or minister is enough for the disaffected to call time on their churchgoing.

Pastoral experience also teaches that even if any necessary fence mending takes place in such circumstances, or if questions of faith and doubt are addressed sensitively and competently, those concerned may still not return to church. Any prior spiritual impetus may have simply run its course, or else some combination of the six Cs that previously maintained their involvement has either failed, been surrendered with relief, or transferred to something more satisfying. Such former churchgoers have become disillusioned, dissatisfied with what is on offer, apathetic, or just plain bored. The set of cultural factors that tells against churchgoing more generally further encourages wavering Christians to become lapsed ones.

All this arises before we get to major scandals that have poisoned the well of Church involvement for many. We in the Church not only failed to attract, but we have now succeeded in driving away a large cohort for good. The last century and a half have seen a stubborn refusal of modern scientific, philosophical, and psychological insights into the world and the human condition, along with resistance to the proper pursuit of human rights and freedoms, both from a strong backward-looking current in Roman Catholicism and from Protestant biblical fundamentalism. Then there are the stubbornly uncaring moralistic positions we have taken while being responsible in many places for appallingly abusive behavior and its institutional coverup. If we behave like an anxiously defensive institution untethered from our spiritual and ethical moorings, no wonder many have come to despise us—and can we entirely blame them? If someone walks into a bank and robs it, it is a crime; but if a bank manager does the robbery, it is a scandal. We have brought a lot of problems on ourselves.

For all that, I still want to make a case for the liturgical, Eucharistic Church and why someone might want to be part of its Sunday-by-Sunday worshipping life in the West—and this while taking today's Western climate of wariness, skepticism, and indifference with appropriate seriousness. I come to this task with conviction; I believe that Jesus Christ is alive in his Church through the Holy Spirit, inviting us to the Lord's table and to an adventurous newness of life that today's world needs to see. With those principles in mind, I will be exploring what the Church has meant, can mean, and should never mean, in the hope that readers might consider re-evaluating it, sticking with it, or even joining it.

About this Book

My claim is that the Eucharistic Church constitutes a necessary and proper context for Christian faith, life, and mission, at a time when that traditional conviction has become largely inexplicable in Western culture. I want to show how the Church is central to God's purposes while facing up to the Church's widely acknowledged problems and its accelerating institutional decline. The book achieves its aim by presenting a cumulative case for the Church as God's healing project in history, as a place where human imagination and characteristic self-defining behaviors are programmatically challenged and transformed, and where institutional failure is faced and acknowledged rather than denied or else projected onto others. The fragile reality of an all-too-human Church is theologically interpreted as the necessary context for a "nontribal tribe" to emerge, which has learned the gospel's lessons of mercy and forgiveness. My approach throughout employs a combination of theological and scriptural reflection along with discussion of contemporary cultural and political realities. I pay attention to the concerns of unaligned and disaffected modern Westerners while questioning today's dominant culture of therapeutic individualism. The book is not a complete ecclesiology nor an academic treatise on secularization nor a how-to-do-it book for growing the Church. It commends a Eucharistic abiding that decenters, forms, and heals the Christian individual, enlisting Christians in the adventure of desiring and hence living differently. My fondest hope is that it might help frustrated and disappointed ecclesial consumers to rediscover themselves as gifted and grateful participants in something more adventurous, and more comradely. The book's argument unfolds in six chapters.

The first chapter, entitled "Church as Hardware," offers three snapshots of situations past and present in which the

Church has been indispensable for imagining and living the Christian life. There is the early period of significant Christian growth, when a uniquely liberating faith and practice made the Church a beacon and a refuge. Then there is the Christendom era in which European societies were structured according to a liturgically enacted Christian cosmology binding all of life together. Finally, we have today's Global South where burgeoning churches provide a crucial context for populations to make demanding socio-economic transitions. Acknowledging sociological approaches, I set out what it looks like when being Christian means being integrally ecclesial.

The second chapter, called "Church as Software," considers what has changed in the modern West so that the Church is no longer considered essential for being Christian. What was *hardware*, making and shaping Christian lives, has become *software*, providing support and optional resources for Christian individuals. I set out the aspects of secularization—the migration of religious functions from the Church to other entities (e.g., the nation state), with religion turned into a separate category alongside other previously unified dimensions of premodern societies. I use Charles Taylor's key terms for explicating how belonging is no longer a given, or indeed anything much else beyond the individual and their perceived needs. Church affiliation and belonging have thus become largely a matter of choice, and even for today's serious Christians. Nevertheless, I affirm the early Dietrich Bonhoeffer's culturally challenging claim that Church attendance is of the essence, and this for theological reasons rather than any consideration of potential personal benefit.

In the third chapter, "Abiding in the Vine," I present the integral nature of Church belonging for life in Christ. I use the heart-based image of systole and diastole to show how the inflow of abiding in Christ leads to the outflow of mission, at a time when many anxious Western churches are turning from abiding to activism. The mission is to spread the fruits of this newfound abiding in peace—of a nonrivalrous and nonviolent identity freed from self-justification. I consider today's culture wars, conspiracy theories, and authoritarian populism, against which the witness of a nontribal tribe is most necessary.

Chapter 4, "Treasures in Earthen Vessels," considers problems in the Church not as the sum of individual Christian wrongs but in more systemic terms. The Holy Church of God is at the same time a flawed human institution. Jesus Christ does not oversee a perfectionist Church entitled to impose an exclusivist version of purity. Instead, he is the friend of sinners. He is the great sign of God's perennial patience with a beloved but recalcitrant people. Indeed, Christ accepts the mantle of sinful outsider so that no sinner need ever feel cursed and abandoned by God.

In Chapter 5, called "Watermarks of the Church," I address this actual, flawed yet graced Church in terms of its four traditional credal marks—one, holy, catholic, and apostolic—which I prefer to regard as *watermarks*: that is, as present though not always readily perceived. I do so in dialog with a range of Reformation-era developments of this theme, along with modern Catholic, Anglican, and ecumenical discussion, to see how the traditional marks might apply to today's settled multiplicity of churches. I show how oneness can be compatible with this multiplicity, sketch an alternative holiness that embraces rather than excludes, and I posit a high-bandwidth Catholicity of principled inclusiveness that favors a "generously orthodox" account of apostolicity. All of this is what one would expect from a nontribal tribe.

The final chapter, entitled "Come and See," reconsiders how people are drawn to the Church. I suggest that at heart it is not about meeting personal needs, cultivating worthwhile experiences, or other culturally favored inducements, but because Christ desires to gather a people to himself out of love for the world. I dwell on Pope Francis's apostolic letter, *Desiderio Desideravi*, about Jesus's earnest desire to eat the Passover with his disciples, along with discussing how this invitation is presented in the Gospels with parables of the treasure and the pearl, in the Emmaus road account, and with the raising of Lazarus. I then survey a range of what I am calling post-Church options. These are newer fellowships that have abandoned churchgoing, including versions springing up online and in virtual reality. I regard these as inadequate vehicles for meeting and being shaped by Jesus Christ.

By the Church and its Eucharistic communities actually *being the Church*—systolic and diastolic—people will be helped to recognize and to claim Jesus's invitation to life in the Church. Some implications for faith that this entails are flagged in the book's Conclusion. A selection of questions is also provided, at the end of each chapter. These are for private reflection or journaling, as pastoral conversation starters or when using the book one-to-one with adult seekers, and whenever *Why Church?* is discussed in book clubs, in Lenten and other Church study groups, in confirmation classes, clergy forums, and in the classroom. In all these cases, while the map provided is mine, the potential adventure is yours.

1

Church as Hardware

Christ be with me, Christ within me,
Christ behind me, Christ before me,
Christ beside me, Christ to win me,
Christ to comfort and restore me.
Christ beneath me, Christ above me,
Christ in quiet, Christ in danger,
Christ in hearts of all that love me,
Christ in mouth of friend and stranger.

"St Patrick's Breastplate" (433AD)
trans. Cecil Francis Alexander

Christianity emerged from the resurrection of Jesus Christ, which was God's great game-changing answer to the power of death and of entrenched human dysfunction. The early Church provided a compelling alternative to what St Augustine called the earthly city,[1] and was later woven together with that earthly city into a Christian civilization. But that was then; this is now. The Church has lost appeal in the modern West and has had to surrender many of its former claims, finding itself increasingly marginal in today's thoroughly autonomous earthly city. More on the nature of that transformation and marginalization in the next chapter. But first let me label the transformation using two terms from the field of computing: hardware and software. In the past, and in some places still, the Church is like *hardware*, while the contemporary Western Church is often more like *software*. Something foundational to Christian faith and practice has become the provider of optional (and hence dispensable) resources.

To illustrate this, I offer three snapshots, two past and one present. They highlight eras and cultural contexts in which the Church and belonging to it made (and makes) perfect sense. The first comes from the Church's early centuries of expansion, after the New Testament period but before Christianity became the established religion of the fourth-century Roman Empire. The second snapshot, from medieval Christendom, points to how Christianity and its Church knitted European civilization together both imaginatively and socially. The third snapshot is non-Western. It comes from today's Global South (chiefly Latin America, Africa, and parts of Asia) where a Christian resurgence is underway and churches are booming. Indeed, Global South Christianity is beginning to influence Northern Hemisphere Church life, in some places reversing its decline.

There are clear parallels between trends in today's Global South and how Christianity caught on in the Church's early centuries. These snapshots show how the Church has built communities ancient and modern, along with a civilization based on an interweaving of Christian beliefs and practices, with ordinary people flocking and clinging to it. We will see that faith was never typically a matter of first being persuaded by Christian truth and only then joining the Church, if at all. Rather, it meant coming to inhabit the reality of a Christian worldview as embodied in a community and its practices. Which of course is no longer how things are seen in the West.

First Snapshot: Early Christian Expansion

The Roman Empire was not famous for its social workers! It was a harsh pagan world in which the Christian Church emerged from its origins in the blessed faith and religious practice of Israel to take its countercultural stand. Why Church? There is a clear answer if Church means deliverance from spiritual oppression, including from hostile and dehumanizing circumstances. So it was for those drawn to the Church in its early centuries of expansion, when being a Christian brought hitherto unimagined blessings.

The American sociologist Rodney Stark takes an empirical approach to the increase of early Christianity without invoking any supernatural cause or advantage. He simply considers how the Church's beliefs about God, Christ, the meaning of history, and what comes after were made manifest in a community that cared for people as if they mattered. This was a new thing. What is more, the embodying of Christian beliefs in the Church made it rational for those who were attracted to the Church and joined it to accept those beliefs.

In his book *The Rise of Christianity*, Stark sets aside the nowadays prevalent view that Christian religion is a matter of groundless fantasy. Instead, he sees early Christian conversion as a sensible choice for rational actors who inhabited a dangerous and troubled geography, culture, and epoch. Stark's approach departs from widespread sociological custom. He believes that it is more scientific to take the facts about early Christian growth seriously, not discounting them in accord with ideological bias. The subtitle of Stark's book—*How the Obscure, Marginal Jesus Movement Became the Dominant Religious Force in the Western World in a Few Centuries*—reflects his sociologist's conviction that early Christian expansion was sufficiently historically distinctive to require an explanation.

In addition to a certain enhanced accessibility that Christianity gained from its affinities with already-existing Hellenistic Judaism (i.e., Judaism's Greek-enculturated development), Stark makes most of the unique practical benefits brought by Christian belief as manifested for Jews and Gentiles through the Church.

So, for instance, in a world where Athenian and Roman women were subject to poor treatment, he suggests that early Christianity brought women a heightened status. Consider, too, how women boosted the numbers by bringing along their husbands as secondary converts. Christian women's numbers also grew because of Christian opposition to the widespread, culturally sanctioned infanticide of girls.

Christians also nursed the sick, including during major pandemics. Stark provides a striking picture of the crowded, unsafe, unsanitary, indeed regularly catastrophic living conditions in cities where Christianity took root. Consequently, the mutual support and health care provided by Church members helped Christians to survive in greater relative numbers, while also attracting converts from the wider community who had received life-saving care.

Christian doctrine helped to foster all these distinctive behaviors, encouraging the formation of Church communities out of diverse ethnic elements that were marked by belonging and mutual service. These new beliefs also supported the witness of martyrdom, which demonstrated a sense of solidarity and honor at odds with the earthly city and its norms. The Church's martyrs had a disquieting effect on the pagans, who recognized no spiritual worth in welcoming suffering, shame, and dishonor. Instead, belief in the cross and resurrection of Jesus Christ told against the pagan empire with its oppressive civil religion and values. Yet only because the Church took this belief seriously and put it to work. Christian beliefs would not otherwise have convinced as many people of their truth. The Church's radically new values and practices were the necessary vector of Christian faith's eventual ascendency in the Roman world. They made the Church's narrative of Jesus Christ visible and credible—at once a sacramental manifestation of the gospel and a practical drawcard.

Christian radical inclusiveness continued to encourage Church growth during subsequent centuries, with bishops regarding the poor as God's people—as brothers and sisters in Christ rather than charity cases.[2] Believers' numbers by the mid-fourth century had grown to represent just over half the by-then officially Christian Empire. But the Church, for all its distinctive influence, inevitably became more caught up with the earthly city. The integration of faith and culture—of the heavenly and earthly cities—came to define the next, long stage of Christian history, which can be regarded as extending up to the sixteenth-century Protestant Reformation and the cusp of modernity. In that extended era, a new symbiosis of Christian believing and Church belonging became established. It was not the later version of Christianity favored by Protestant Reformers, with their preference for unmediated personal faith in tune with emerging currents of modern individualism. But it did represent a reinvention of integral Christian belonging, and from that era comes our next snapshot.

Second Snapshot: A Bygone Christian Civilization

We have seen that belonging to the early Church offered some respite from dehumanizing spiritual conditions, with new beliefs and a new collective reality marked by compassionate solidarity. While remaining within the earthly city and not immune from its influence, as St Augustine recognized, the Church's true home was God's heavenly city. Participating in this transition from earth to heaven through the Church was the meaning of salvation. Spiritual attitudes and practical conditions in the earthly city of the pagans helped make clear to Christians what the absence of that salvation looked like, providing the context in which converts sought refuge in the Church through faith and baptism.

Things were different in Europe once the civilization had become demonstrably Christian. Under this newer Christendom, one normally came to the Church through birth and infant baptism, followed by nurture within a communal ritual framework manifesting a generally accepted Christian cosmology. Every cosmology situates human existence within a broader account of what is in the world and why, how continuity and change are related, how everyday life and ultimate human ends are held together, and how divine involvement is to be understood, all serving to locate persons and communities in a meaningful whole.

Christianity had of course always made cosmological claims. If you read the New Testament epistles and Gospels looking for such claims you will quickly find them—from God's cosmos-constituting Word becoming human flesh (John 1:1–5, 14), for a while made lower than the supposed cosmic angelic hierarchy (Hebrews 2:7–9), to Jesus's Epiphany with its obedient guiding star (Matthew 2:1–2, 9–10), to many nature miracles throughout the Gospels, to Jesus's triumphant Ascension into heaven (Acts 1:9, 1 Peter 3:22), to the Church's mission to the "powers and principalities" thought to run the cosmos (Ephesians 3:10–11, Colossians 2:15), to the seer of the Book of Revelation whose vision of a world put right ends the Bible. But in the Christendom era, the cosmological implications of the gospel were developed to shape a whole civilization.

The prevailing cosmology under Christendom was indebted to a compelling synthesis of Greek philosophical schools from late antiquity called Neo-Platonism. It saw all of reality brought together by God within a hierarchy of being. This vision was visibly expressed through the paired aristocratic and ecclesiastical hierarchies structuring the Kingdom and the Church. The English sociologist Martin Stringer explains how deeply rooted and widespread this comprehensive Christian vision of reality had become. In that bygone world, he writes,

> Christian discourses are dominant not simply because they are espoused by the elite, political and ecclesial, but because they form the commonsense, everyday, cosmological discourses within which everybody has to function. Christianity, by the eleventh century, had for most of Europe, and a few places beyond, formed the basic cosmology or worldview of the vast majority of the population. This cosmology was fundamentally different from that of the pagan societies that it had usurped, and it differed subtly from one society to another. This cosmology, however, this commonsense view of how the world worked and what the world consisted of, was fundamentally Christian ... and rooted in the official forms and structures of worship as practiced at this time.[3]

Against this widely accepted imaginative backdrop, faith was not characteristically a matter of choosing something new let alone alien. Nor were these Christians seeking refuge from the world in the Church—unless that refuge was from the worst of worldly temptations, in the supposedly higher spiritual state of life that a monastery or convent provided. Otherwise, Christendom-era faith represented less of an alternative to the reigning priorities. Sovereigns and nobles, merchants and peasants, clergy and lay people, saints and sinners, monks, nuns, and profligates all belonged to the one Church and shared its prevailing cosmology. They may have been more-or-less faithful Christians—that is, their faith may have been subjectively inhabited to a greater or lesser extent, which today's more personally oriented Christian perspective would regard as the most significant consideration.

But Christians they remained, whether good ones or bad, as part of a Christian civilization. The development of a society-wide Christian cosmological framework situated the personal dimension of their faith, though without necessarily supplanting it.

The primary role of formal worship and its rituals according to this cosmological faith was to preserve order and stability in the cosmos. "Here was a Christianity that spoke less about individual conversion and concerns about the end of the world, and more about the maintenance of the world and being drawn up into the glory of God."[4] Stringer shows how this played out in two great cathedrals, one Eastern and the other Western (representing what were then the Church's two halves, separated since 1054).

At the Cathedral of Hagia Sophia in Kyiv, as previously in Constantinople, the church building, its divisions, and its furnishings represented the cosmos figuratively, while the Eucharist celebrated under its heavenly dome was understood to re-enact the life of Christ that linked heaven and earth. The beauty of this great Eastern church evoked the beauty of heaven, with earthly voices joining the heavenly choir of angels, while the paintings and icons showed participants in the earthly Eucharist that they had come into the heavenly courts.

In Salisbury, the Western cathedral's characteristically cruciform shape evoked a cosmos centered on Christ. Likewise, its Latin liturgy followed the Western emphasis on Christ's sacrificial death, pleaded before the heavenly throne at a main daily Eucharist along with perhaps twenty private masses celebrated by priests at side altars, though often before lay onlookers. Cathedral canons maintained a rhythm of daily offices so that prayer reliably went up from the cathedral hour by hour and day by day. As Stringer explains,

This is worship undertaken by a clerical elite, worship with fully detailed and carefully controlled ceremonial and ritual, worship whose sole function is the maintenance of the world as it is. Without this worship, demanded of us by God, then the whole creation would groan and grind to a halt. Along with this cosmological understanding of worship came a sense of the punishment of God in plagues and famine, a close link between the fortunes of the nation and the worship of the people, and a realization of the vagaries of nature. All of creation is brought into the worship and that worship provides the powerhouse of faith that maintains the world in its course.[5]

It is such worship that bound together the devotional and communal life of Christians, and especially in the Eucharist.

The life of rural communities was centered on the village church and shaped by rituals that bound genders and social strata together along with their faithfully commemorated dead. The Church's cycle of annual seasons and religious festivals, with accompanying fêtes and processions, sanctified the seasonal rhythms of rural life. Rites of confession and of deathbed absolution and communion (in England called "shrift and housel"), along with regularly seeing the priest elevate the sacred host at mass in the meantime, helped keep Christians at peace with God, their consciences, and among themselves. A number of ritual practices later rejected by Protestant Reformers as pagan superstition were actually highly valued signs of Christ's presence and power throughout the world to ward off evil—a power thought to abide in certain charms and relics, specific prayers, and priestly actions.

As the revisionist English historian Eamon Duffy shows in his magisterial work on the coherent Christian reality present in England before the Reformation, and how reluctantly it was eventually let go by much of the population, the Reform-ers were wrong that Christ's centrality was denied in medieval Catholicism. The medieval Christ did, however, work through a spiritually charged cosmos to maintain a web of Christian belonging in villages, towns, and the whole realm.[6] Sociol-ogy and theology were woven fine, as in the early Church, but in a very different way. The journey from the earthly to the heavenly city now took place within a Christian cosmology, in a Christian realm that updated the early Church's solidarity, and all of it united in Jesus Christ. Of course, faith was per-sonal as well as cosmological before the English Reformation and it did not want for devotion. Though it was not recogniz-ably modern, and it was certainly not Evangelical Protestant. But thereafter, as Roger Haight nicely puts it, "The institu-tional Church changed around the corporate body of English Christians."[7]

Third Snapshot: Global South Churches Today

According to the American historian of religion Philip Jenkins, 83% of the world's Christians in the year 1900 lived in Europe, while it is projected that by 2050, 72% will live in Africa, Asia, and Latin America.[8] That is, in the Global South. Likewise, it is predicted that in 2050 a billion people, or one in ten, will be Pentecostal Christians. As Elle Hardy points out in her global survey of Pentecostalism, a quarter of the world's Christians are now Pentecostals, up from 6% in 1980.[9] This major trans-formation has been described as a new Reformation.

These numbers do not strictly overlap, as the numer-ous newer African Independent Churches are neither all nor wholly Pentecostal. Carrying over syncretistic aspects of the traditional African religions from which many of them emerged, these indigenous groups tend to accept interac-tion with benign spiritual beings. And they do not share the traditional Western Christian stress on sin and guilt.[10] Pentecostals, however, differ strongly on both counts, and they typically come out of existing mainstream churches rather than straight from paganism.

In any event, the emphasis throughout emerging Global South churches is on spiritual deliverance from evil forces that oppress humanity, including their manifestation in adverse social conditions, injustice, racism, economic disadvantage, and other unfortunate legacies of colonialism. In Africa, this means deliverance from sickness and poverty as much as from sorcery and evil spirits.[11] "Taking all these threats together—disease, exploitation, pollution, drink, drugs, and violence—it is easy to see why people might easily accept that they were under siege from demonic forces, and that only divine intervention could save them."[12]

This supernaturally haunted mindset can strike Western Christians as primitive, simplistic, and even sub-Christian, with its exorcisms, prophetic testimony, dream visions, and apocalyptic predictions. However, criticisms flow both ways. Global South churches readily condemn Western Christianity for embracing secular liberalism, especially when Western churches are becoming more open-minded and nonjudgmental on same-sex issues.[13] Many African Christians, however, have not forgotten how missionaries refused to accept their traditional polygamous practices in favor of Western-style monogamy. Today's postcolonial sensitivities ensure that further attempts to import what are perceived to be alien cultural practices from the Global North will be resisted. Former colonial masters are no longer welcome to set the agenda, with pressure to accept same-sex relationships becoming a flashpoint in churches of the Global South.

Yet their appeal remains strong. In the same way that early churches grew by caring for their members while attracting outsiders through practical solicitude and welcome new attitudes, Jenkins explains that in today's Global South,

> Churches provide a refuge during a time of immense and barely comprehensible social change.... [Their] sense of family and fellowship is crucial for understanding the wide and remarkably diverse appeal of new Christian congregations.... The churches provide a social network that would otherwise be lacking and help teach members the skills they need to survive in a rapidly developing society.[14]

Indeed, the veteran English sociologist David Martin describes Pentecostalism as a key modern vehicle for fostering prosperity in the developing world—not by supernatural means, but simply by instilling the attitudes, values, and disciplines necessary for equipping poor and uneducated workers to join a modernizing economy and workforce.[15] It is a nice irony that what could be regarded as a decidedly nonmodern version of Christian belief actually underwrites modernization through socio-economic transformation.

If the expanding Church of the early centuries combined an emancipatory theological vision with concrete liberating practices, so-called dissenting churches such as the Methodists did the same during Britain's Industrial Revolution. They reached out to a displaced rural workforce facing wretched social and working conditions in overcrowded urban centers.[16] Such alternative Church communities provided a support network, hope, and belonging for those consigned to William Blake's "dark Satanic Mills." And many such churches continue to provide this witness and service among the poor and struggling in today's West. But it is a major feature of the Church in today's Global South.

We see it, too, as Global South Christians emigrate to the Northern Hemisphere in search of a better life. They are already beginning to revitalize churches and communities in places more accustomed to Church decline. This might suggest the possibility of a stronger future for European Christianity. Although it will look very different, not least by becoming blacker and browner. "When we measure the declining strength of Christianity in Europe," as Jenkins points out, "we must remember how much leaner the statistics would be if not for recent immigrants and their children—the new Europeans."[17]

Finally, I reflect that today's modest revival of European Church numbers under Global South influence might not be the end of the story. A larger-scale Western Church resurgence is conceivable if social and economic conditions were to decline precipitately. In the sort of apocalyptic scenario that is already being imagined in fiction and film, the social fabric could collapse to leave whole populations exposed and desperate. For instance, climate change and allied catastrophes—such as the sudden failure of a key climate-stabilizing ocean current like the North Atlantic Conveyor, or even the Gulf Stream—could conceivably overcome the defenses of Western society. This might well unleash unimagined new pandemics, vast hordes of climate refugees, major temperature-induced crop failure, supply chain collapse, the inundation of coastal cities due to melting ice caps, and then major new wars (fought to secure scarce resources, perhaps, or else to seize new advantages). One might imagine the Western Church recovering itself as it rises to the challenge of widespread social and economic collapse, though one can also imagine appalling Christian variants wreaking havoc under such conditions in the hands of authoritarian populists.

In its early centuries of expansion, in premodern European Christian civilization, in today's Global South and perhaps again (sooner or later) in the face of a global civilizational crisis, the question "Why Church" finds a straightforward answer. But that is not the case in today's West. Today's churchgoers in the West might still look for personal support, especially when life is something of a struggle. They might value the experience of community that congregational involvement offers when facing the loneliness of urban anonymity or old age. The Church might provide opportunities and resources for empowerment, creativity, and service, from its committees to its choirs to its community outreach projects. One might be noticed, befriended, and cared for at church, regardless of whatever is happening up the front in worship. And of course, the Church might provide a measure of meaning and orientation through its liturgical life, preaching, and study groups (if only to reinforce existing social values). But none of this is quite the world-transforming alternative that early Christianity provided and that we can still find in Global South churches, just as the meaning and belonging on offer in today's Western churches is not the same as abiding in that bygone shared cosmos under the overarching sign of Christ. For good or ill, things are just different now.

The Church—no longer seen in the West as either a heaven-sent refuge or else the pivot on which a whole cosmology turns—is increasingly consigned to niche service provision in the religious sector of our highly diversified secular modern world. In the next chapter, I will content myself with a descriptive approach rather than seeking to trace the multistranded back story of these developments. What matters is to get a sense of the imaginative world in which the Church now finds itself, and which is also found in the Church.

For Reflection and Discussion

- We see how crucial the Church was for Christians in past eras, and still is in the Global South. Is the Church crucial for us? Why or why not?

- Do you feel nostalgic for bygone forms of the Church, or are they best left in the past?

- If global conditions get a lot worse and Western civilization collapses, could a reinvigorated Church emerge? What might a post-apocalyptic Church look like?

CHAPTER

2

Church as Software

We asked a series of questions. What drew you to the church? What do you like best? . . . If you come to church only occasionally—why is that? (My biggest concern.) To which several answered: We love the church. We love being members. But church isn't our only Sunday priority. . . . Which poses the question: how can we *be* church for *these* people?

Rev Terry Elsberry
Leading With Love:
Essentials of Church Leadership, 199.

The lack of a compelling need for the Church typifies secular modernity in the West. For most people, the thought of any Church involvement—beyond attending weddings, funerals, and increasingly rare "christenings"— simply never arises. And this is often a matter of disinterest rather than one of conscientious disbelief. Clearly, belonging to the Church in the West is no longer the rational choice that it represented in the early centuries of Christian expansion and remains in churches of the Global South.

The Christendom pattern of Church belonging has also passed away. It centered on sharing a cosmos, while serious Christian practice in today's West looks more like choosing an option or perhaps staking out a position. The sort of Church involvement that served as a valued marker of national heritage or cultural identity is correspondingly on the wane. This represented a survival of the Christendom mindset, but it is evaporating in an increasingly global and multicultural era. So, for instance, Catholic Church attendance is collapsing in Poland, while as recently as in the 1980s it was an anchor of solidarity against communism. Likewise in Quebec numbers at mass are now relatively lower than elsewhere in Canada, despite Catholic identity having once counted for much among French-speaking Québécois with separatist aspirations. Take away the Church's heightened sociological function, and the limited contribution of genuine believing Christian commitment is revealed.

In this second chapter, I begin with a section entitled "Beyond Belonging," about how secularization has reshaped our modern West. It has disarticulated society's varied aspects that were once united through an overarching Christian cosmology, which includes reducing the scope of religious belief and practice to a distinct sphere of human activity. Under these secular conditions, some former sociological functions of religion have migrated to other aspects of modern Western life, from the nation state to the linked obsessions of consumerism and romantic love to the sports field, offering some of the transcendence otherwise missing from secular life. All this has left us with a more-or-less restless individualism in search of consoling narratives, with organized religion now widely seen as providing resources for a dwindling minority of consumers. The cultural window in our modern West has closed on being able to regard anything communal as primary, and necessarily formative, rather than secondary, helpfully supportive perhaps, but ultimately optional. This section will cover a lot of ground in short order and will feel denser than what went before and comes after.

Then, in a section called "Choosing Church," on the consequences of these social changes for Church involvement, I will look at how yesterday's integral Christian belonging has morphed into the optional following of a personal spiritual itinerary—how a Church that was once *hardware* has now become *software*. As the American sociologist Robert

Wuthnow explains, it is because "a traditional spirituality of inhabiting has given way to a new spirituality of seeking—that people have been losing faith in a metaphysic that can make them feel at home in the universe and that they increasingly negotiate among competing glimpses of the sacred, seeking partial knowledge and practical wisdom."[1] This newer privatizing and instrumentalizing agenda, along with the Church's numerical decline, reflects today's hegemony of choice. Indeed, even belonging to the Church today demands a choice. Once it was the heretics who chose, but now it is the orthodox believers.[2]

Beyond Belonging

In his magisterial discussion, *A Secular Age*, the Canadian historian of ideas Charles Taylor provides four idioms for describing what has become of us in the modern West: there is the *porous* self, contrasted with the *buffered* self, then the *nova* and the *immanent frame*. In the Christendom era, the self was more *porous*, blended into a larger world of meaning, and part of something given. Since then, the self has become more bounded, more *buffered* as Taylor prefers to put it. It is a self that is more like a gated community than an open-access suburb—it is no longer porous.

Looking back to the old cosmology and then around at what little remains of it in the West, Taylor explains that the older "porous self is vulnerable, to spirits, demons, cosmic forces. And along with this go certain fears which can grip it in certain circumstances." Whereas today's "buffered self can form the ambition of disengaging from whatever is beyond the boundary, and of giving its own kind of autonomous order to its life."[3] The sense of inhabiting an order of heavenly grace that bound society together from within—structuring the lives of individuals and communities through participation in

sacred rituals along the sanctified timeline of a liturgical year—
has given way in modernity. Instead, the public world is now
constituted simply by the human actions taking place within
it, while the affirmation of everyday life apart from any lofty
spiritual agenda has increasingly come to characterize Western
sensibility.[4]

This shift in worldview is what Taylor calls the *nova*, referring to the transition from Christendom's world of coherent
believing and belonging to today's riot of spiritual options.
Yesterday's set menu has been replaced by today's lavish (if not
uniformly nutritious) buffet. As Taylor explains,

> the intervening centuries have seen the dissipation
> of the enchanted cosmos (some elements of belief in
> enchantment remain, but they don't form a system,
> and are held by individuals here and there, rather than
> being socially shared). Then there came the introduc-
> tion, within the context of the modern moral order,
> of a viable alternative to belief, of forms of exclusive
> humanism, in turn followed by the multiplication of
> both believing and unbelieving positions, which I have
> called the "nova." This all generated the challenge,
> undermining, and dissolution of the early social forms
> which embedded God's presence in social space.[5]

It is not as if the buffered self is closed to belief, or unable
to be moved by anything—for instance, by the beauties of
nature and art.[6] It is just that nature is no longer as reliably
relatable to the supernatural, while art makes its appeal inde-
pendently of any agreed-upon traditional template or transcendent form. So, while signals of transcendence certainly
remain, they are like the tiny ferromagnets in iron that will
only line up in a uniform direction when there is something to
magnetize them. The widely shared Christian cosmology once
provided such a magnetic field, but no longer.

Last to be mentioned among Taylor's four idioms is the *immanent frame*, which refers to how we occupy these new conditions without our former cosmological bearings. This is now a world that we make, largely for our own ends, with nothing of compelling significance determining what those ends should be. For Taylor, "the buffered identity of the disciplined individual moves in a constructed social space where instrumental rationality is a key value, and time is pervasively secular. All this makes up what I want to call 'the immanent frame'."[7] This instrumental rationality can be defined as behaving in the world so that you get exactly what you most want, given the resources available to you. Put more technically, we could characterize instrumental rationality as the optimization of the individual's goal fulfillment.

If that sounds familiar, it is because it represents the guiding principle by which much of the West lives, vastly different from that bygone world where God in Christ determined human meaning and obligations. To live according to instrumental rationality has been called spiritually shallow and materialistic, though there are still currents of belief at play that prevent our modern West from sinking entirely into godless materialism. Taylor describes this in terms of "cross pressure" from belief and unbelief. These are not separate realms, therefore, but features of all modern experience that will forever be jostling together.[8] Indeed, modern constructive theology is full of what would have been called unbelief in the premodern Church.

Protestantism advanced the spiritual evacuation of a unified Christian cosmology and marked the end of a single authoritative Church in the West. Protestant movements were more-or-less open to the Catholic past—the Reformation in England and Sweden, for instance, preserved more traditional marks of faith and order than was the case elsewhere in Europe. Yet the general Protestant trend was toward more direct and unmediated personal access to God, with the sacraments relegated to a supporting role.

At its extreme, this shift saw God's presence in the world retreating to the pages of an authoritative Bible, which spoke into an effectively secular space. Some Protestants, in the tradition of Huldrych Zwingli (1484–1531), were insistent in their abandonment of the medieval sacramental worldview, replacing the Eucharist as saving mystery with the Lord's Supper understood as devout remembrance. Emptied sanctuaries and whitewashed church walls point to an imaginative split being enjoined at the radical end of this new movement. It meant turning inward from a shared world to a supposedly purer and certainly more articulate Christianity, in which believing preceded belonging.

Protestant churches shifted away from being the spiritual mother of Christians to become what the Anglican *Book of Common Prayer*, in its communion rite, called "the blessed company of all faithful people." That is, the Church became less a body constituted from above and more a fellowship entered into from below—a *social contract*; a human community deriving from godly individuals. This pattern also appeared in the new English commonwealth as conceived by Thomas Hobbes (1588–1679) in his book *Leviathan* (1651), with individuals preceding the community. What for the medieval Church and cosmology had been a gift of belonging now became a matter of joining and remaking the Church.

This was the imaginative climate in which individualism overtook community, making it secondary and derivative in the West. In his helpful historical treatment of this shift, Frank Kirkpatrick describes the consequences of an inversion that has largely swept all before it. He concludes rather unfavorably that "the dominant characteristic of persons remains their self-interest and consequent disinterest in others, a disinterest or diffidence to which even the feelings of union or fellow feelings remain subordinate."[9] Accordingly, for Kirkpatrick, and with clear implications for the Church's prospects, "whatever communities of love and trust emerge from these conditions must necessarily . . . be fragile, contingent, and derivative. They cannot be complete or fulfill human nature: they can, at best, provide a diversion or an enjoyment for it over and above what it needs to be itself."[10]

Following its eclipse there were various attempts to match the once-powerful symbol system of religion, with the aim of knitting society together and enlisting popular support as religion once did.[11] Kirkpatrick observes that Karl Marx (1818–1883) was one of the first who tried to overcome the deficiencies of modernity's atomistic approach to being human with something more organic, though of course without God. It is as if God's old functions and attributes were passed on to humanity, which must thereafter create the world by itself.[12] It is interesting that the Church and communism represented rival challenges to the erasure of foundational communal obligations, and to the loss of an overarching sense that history is meaningful. Indeed, in the century between its two Vatican Councils the Roman Catholic Church was dominated at every level by opposition to modernity in general but to communism's "alternative Church" in particular (though, in terms of its social teaching, Rome was also critical of capitalist excesses).[13]

The migration of the religious functions to new entities in the modern West represents one aspect of secularization. Chief among these entities was the new nation state. This shift accompanied the increasing privatization and individualization of religion typifying the sixteenth-century Protestant Reformation, which helped to keep religious claims and sanctions out of a public arena that had been ceded to nation states. The sacred aura that some modern nations have arrogated to themselves illustrates the point. We saw it under Nazism. We see it now with Putin's warmongering claims on behalf of "Holy

Russia." And we see it in Trump's cult-like MAGA version of American Christian nationalism. In recent historical scholarship, William T. Cavanaugh has developed this reading of secularization with his book *Migrations of the Holy*. As he assesses the American case, there has been "a shift from a nation under God to a nation as God's incarnation on earth."[14] Indeed, he concludes that "America has become a new Church."[15] So, secularization is not the end of religious functioning as much as its migration.

The other leading definition of secularization focusses on how modern societies have reified and diversified their key functions. A once-cohesive, socio-religious whole is now a multisector society comprised of government, bureaucracy, infrastructure, industry, business, finance, agriculture, health, education, science, technology, entertainment—and religion. Religion continues, and of course spirituality is on everyone's lips, but without any overall inspirational or coordinating function. The American sociologist José Casanova, in championing this understanding of secularization, describes "societal modernization as a process of functional differentiation and emancipation of the secular spheres—primarily the state, the economy and science—from the religious sphere and the concomitant differentiation and specialization of religion within its newly found religious sphere."[16]

The result is not only the privatizing of religion but also its volatilizing so that, from private centers in the individual and in groups contracted by individuals, religion can contribute to whatever attitudes and practices individuals choose to adopt. There is nothing to rein in this deregulation of religious meaning short of peer influence, which is now significantly mediated through social media. Where once the Church anchored a religious cosmology in the West, now there is a free for all.

A very common attitude in today's West is to regard religious beliefs as metaphors and stories to promote the human good.[17] This is an attitude found within the Church, too, chiefly among mainstream, liberal-tending clergy, congregations, and churchgoers whose approach to doctrine and Church belonging is more typically functional and expressive. This is also a major current in postmodern theology, long championed by Don Cupitt in England and by several liberal Protestant thinkers in the United States. It regards religion in general, and Christianity in particular, as valuable chiefly for helping to cultivate a good and satisfying life apart from any claims for objective truthfulness let alone authority. As the American theologian George Lindbeck describes the liberal churches of his own country, "Like society at large, they are becoming heterogeneous collections of special interest groups united, if at all, by bureaucratic management. Transmitting even a modicum of communal ties and creedal commitment is increasingly left to conservatives. The center is not holding."[18]

Yet conservative Christianity is also implicated in this newer culture of religious deregulation, where a darker side is revealed. We see it emerging in Western Christianity under the influence of fundamentalism and Pentecostalism wherever they contribute to conspiracy theory-fueled authoritarian populism and religious nationalism—in Hungary, Brazil, in the reactionary Orthodoxy of Putin's Russian imperialism, but chiefly in the United States. And of course, these extreme positions are just as postmodern, just as epistemologically nonfoundational, and just as knowingly contemptuous of publicly acknowledged rationality as any questionable beliefs associated with the New Age movement, the less judgmental end of the wellness industry, and with ideological extremes of some progressive movements.

So, whereas some use religious resources to help them be more loving and positive, others use religious resources to help them deny plain reality and stoke hatefulness. Spiritual warfare, as understood by the more isolationist MAGA version of American cultural and religious exceptionalism, has little to do with recognizable Christian tradition and scriptural interpretation, which is about the good news of God in Christ, and everything to do with stockpiling weapons (both ideological and actual) for violent self-definitional conflict—identity politics on steroids.

Instead of fostering the good, according to the kinder, gentler style of postmodern religious belief and practice, this more violent-tending version refuses to acknowledge any wider obligation—to the rule of law, to the common good, to human wellbeing. Witness the huge outpouring of extremist contempt for their fellow citizens shown during the COVID crisis by militant mask refusers and antivaxxers, then with that lethal anti-Epiphany on 6 January 2021 at the United States Capitol. In both cases, angry mobs were fuelled by entirely deregulated though supposedly Christian rhetoric, as magnified in key mainstream and social media echo chambers.

The British sociologist Steve Bruce traces today's falling away from any sort of anchored, shared, and settled reasonableness.

> Once culture was defined by experts. Now we accept the freedom of personal taste. I may not know much about art, but I know what I like. In the late 1960s, claims for personal autonomy moved to a second stage of matters of personal behavior: I may not know much about ethics and morals but I know what I like to do and claim my right to do it. In the third stage, the same attitude is applied to areas of expert knowledge. I may not know much about the nervous system but I know what I like to believe in and I believe in chakras and Shiatsu massage and acupuncture.[19]

Before all this, with the embrace of a Christian cosmology, the moral order was grounded in God's will as then perceived in the complementary testimonies of nature and scripture. What Rowan Williams called the iconic eye was present in the sensibility of that bygone world, helping to maintain accountability—the Eastern Orthodox icon is not only viewed, but it also fixes its eye on the viewer. Now, however, we have lost that iconic eye. An unprecedented level of shamelessness has emerged with the vanishing of an objective reality that is external to our own self-creation and that can both offer us grace and call us into judgment.[20]

"For many people today," then, as Charles Taylor points out, "to conform to some external authority just doesn't seem comprehensible as a form of spiritual life."[21] In particular, as observed by American sociologist Robert Bellah in his influential study of individualism and commitment in America, today's fundamentally individualistic understanding of human life (what he calls ontological individualism) makes it hard to understand the idea that the Church is somehow prior to the believer.[22] This concern will be taken up in the next section, which considers some ways in which these transformed conditions in the West have influenced believing and belonging in the Church.

Choosing Church

It is not as if choice only began to influence Church involvement from early modern times. St Paul (1 Corinthians 1:12, 3:4) had to deal with competing factions, as one example of a wider New Testament theme. Later, the move toward settled creeds, fixed orders of ministry and the emergence of Rome's bishop as a figure of unity was a response to heretical currents here and there that led Christians away from the undivided Church. Hence the Latin axiom *extra ecclesiam nulla salus*—outside the Church no salvation—which came from St Cyprian of Carthage in the third century. It expressed the conviction that sticking with the undivided Church in the face of heretical movements was properly Christian, and what God expected. A single Church at peace was meant to stand out in a world dominated by divisive violence and violent association, with its eyes on salvation and the heavenly city even if its feet remained in the earthly one. So, yes, there was individual choice for some, but it was deemed valid in one direction only, and nothing like the situation in today's spiritual marketplace.

In sixteenth-century Europe, however, it became more widely possible for Church affiliation to be chosen. Nations chose because sovereigns chose, likewise reforming intellectuals and their clergy followers chose, while to some extent ordinary people chose. One Church as the sole ark of salvation ceased to be an unquestioned principle. A new Latin axiom took over: *cuius regio, eius religio*—whose realm, their religion—meaning that the religion of the ruler was to dictate the religion of those ruled. Thus, the Protestant Reformation brought denominations into the Church—though originally to a limited extent, and likely chosen by the local prince.

In time, however, many versions of Protestantism divided and separated in pursuit of apparently irreconcilable goals, beyond the relatively stable Lutheran and more traditional Reformed families with their higher view of visible unity. Indeed, Evangelical and Pentecostal Church affiliation is more likely to be functional rather than substantive, with Evangelical or Pentecostal identity and the para-Church groups supporting it often providing primary allegiance (e.g., Samaritan's Purse, interVarsity Christian Fellowship, Billy Graham Evangelistic Association, Scripture Union, Church Missionary Society, Youth with a Mission/YWAM). Their churches' role is often limited to resourcing private faith, devotion, and missionary outreach. For example, some Evangelical Anglicans apologize for their Church not being as Reformed as they would like by justifying it as "a good boat to fish from."

This entirely functional ecclesiology represents another dimension of the Church's transformation into software. Accordingly, as the great twentieth-century Catholic theologian Henri de Lubac lamented,

> the experience of Protestantism should serve as a sufficient warning. Having stripped it of all its mystical attributes, it acknowledged in the visible church a mere secular institution; as a matter of course it abandoned it to the patronage of the state and sought a refuge for the spiritual life in an invisible church, its concept of which had evaporated into an abstract ideal.[23]

This arises, as Friedrich Schleiermacher pointed out, because "[Protestantism] makes the individual's relation to the Church dependent on his relation to Christ, while [Catholicism] contrariwise makes the individual's relation to Christ dependent on his relation to the Church."[24] Protestantism must, therefore, entail some deemphasizing of the Church in the Christian understanding of salvation.

A further factor, which became more significant in Protestant thought during the Enlightenment and then the colonial era, was the recognition and hence the challenge of other world religions. Hinduism, Buddhism, and Confucian philosophy dominated vast territories where Christianity was either little known or had made only modest inroads thanks to Catholic missionary outreach and the beginnings of European colonial expansion. Educated opinion in the Enlightenment readily saw this newfound diversity as further evidence that Christian faith and the Church's spiritual authority were Western constructs, so that universal moral goals could be fostered by whichever local religious tradition. Indeed, the newly isolated and privatized category of religion served to gather up all such forms, only one of which was Christianity. European intellectuals began to translate sacred texts from India, with this turn to the East becoming a marker of 1960s-era social revolution. The new world of religious pluralism was inescapably one of choice.

A major consequence of religion becoming a matter of choice has been a decline in Western Christian affiliation, along with church attendance. This falling-off is beginning to seem like a complete rout in some contexts (e.g., more so in secular Australia than in the stronger cultural afterglow of American civil religiousness). But how is it best characterized? Does it represent a decline in belief and piety, or is it somehow different from that? Does it point to a collapse of private religious commitment, or was that commitment missing in the first place, with new conditions and opportunities at last allowing people to give up something that their heart was never really in? In other words, does it reveal preexisting apathy rather than dwindling conviction?[25] Or is it mimetic? As the German sociologist of religion Detlef Pollack observes, referring to both Protestant and Catholic decline in his country, "When the majority of society belongs to a Church, you have to justify leaving it. But when half the population does not belong to any of these churches, the social pressure drops, and it becomes easier to leave. . . . Instead, you now have to justify why you remain in a Church."[26] To make such a choice— to abandon Christianity, or at least the Church—would not occur in the same way according to any of the three historical snapshots from my first chapter. Now, however, the Church as hardware has become subject to the vicissitudes of choice and is becoming software.

Consider the prompt readiness with which churchgoing is abandoned in certain contexts. One thinks of the young who abandon the Church when they are old enough to begin setting their own course in life, including the vast majority of those who attended church-run schools in Australia. Then there is the decline now being registered in Australian, English, and

American Anglican parishes following lengthy COVID lockdowns. For long months on end, places of worship were closed,
during which time it was either livestreaming (perhaps con-
necting with a more interesting worship environment and its
livestream for the duration) or else nothing. With the eventual
opportunity to return, a significant number have declined to
avail themselves of it. Two further illustrations make the point
clearly, revealing that this trend is not only a matter of drift
but also one of active refusal—although it is important to note
exactly what is and what is not being refused.

Charles Taylor gives the example of a twentieth-century
Breton parish that secularized far more quickly than wider
trends in Catholic France would have predicted. The numbers
fell off precipitately once traditional forms of life and social
expectations in that rural community slackened,[27] suggesting
that churchgoing was part of a cultural package rather than
a faith commitment. Hence, churchgoing was readily abandoned when that package came apart.

Scottish historian Callum Brown makes a similar case for
Christian Britain as a whole, rejecting the established idea that
secularization has been a slow if inexorable process. He concludes from the evidence that Christian practice began its serious collapse in Britain with enhanced emancipation of women
from the 1950s.[28] As a whole way of life centered on the
cultivation of values like reserve, modesty, thrift, and self-ef-
facement began to give way, and especially from the swing-
ing sixties, women *en masse* rejected their culturally mandated
role as standard bearers for these values, including as society's
designated civilizers of men. Everyone was opting for personal
freedom, with women leading the way. Church involvement
declined, therefore, as Church-endorsed bonds of social con-
formity were loosened.

We can largely applaud this release of Christianity and
Church attendance from the stifling grip of respectability,

but the price of this welcome liberation was the emptying of churches—for good or ill. Many took that path out the Church's door from laudable conviction, seeking a more humane and affirming vision of life. But the resulting exodus was not just about getting out from under. The Canadian Presbyterian theologian Gary Badcock is unsparing in his assessment of how a new culture of liberal individualism leads those he calls hungry sheep away from the Church in droves because "they can find the same thing (and it is the same thing) in more convincing forms from the other available consumerist alternatives that equally serve the end of individual flourishing: popular culture, environmental activism, uninhibited sex, the fulfillment of career ambition, politics, or even crass materialism."[29]

There is a particular consumerist logic at work here that has come to prominence in the Western imagination, severely limiting what Christian faith and its ecclesial manifestation can be seen to represent. It is the logic of the hobby and the pastime. As the American Catholic theologian Nicholas Healy observes, "It would be utterly irrational for me to claim that my decision for fishing rather than basketball is one that everyone should follow. Religious decisions are roughly similar. To live a life of witness to Jesus Christ as if his cross *really* had universal significance is irrational and fanatical."[30]

Given such conditions, maintaining the disciplined commitment of regular worship in a mainstream liturgical Church is now very much a choice. For many of the committed it still represents belonging, but it can be a belonging that has to be sustained against counter-pressure. Dietrich Bonhoeffer the martyr reflected on this challenge early on, which he took to be about loving the actual Church over some preferred ideal of the Church.[31] Hence his reaction against judgmental spiritual selectivity in favor of ordinary, persistent churchgoing. Bonhoeffer's early work *Sanctorum Communio* emphasizes the importance of putting up with the flawed reality of a tangible,

concrete congregation. Here he allows his theological judgment to supersede sociological judgment, taking us beyond
today's logic of choice. "Since I belong to the church-community," the young Bonhoeffer insists, "I come to the assembly; this is the simple rationale of those who are assembled.
This act is not based on utilitarian considerations, or a sense
of duty, but is 'organic' and obvious behavior. ... A Christian who stays away from the assembly is a contradiction in
terms."[32]

Bonhoeffer is well aware that this integrally ecclesial
understanding of Christian existence is countercultural and
counterintuitive, just as his picture of what we might find in
the Church assembly is unflatteringly realistic. Despite the
intervening century, his observations strike a decidedly contemporary note:

> Of course, this answer will not satisfy the individual-
> istic inquirer. For cannot each member of the church-
> community read the Bible on their own, and in private
> profess that they belong to the church-community,
> namely the invisible church of the "conscience" and the
> "soul"? What is the purpose of the deadly boredom of
> a publicly visible assembly in which one risks sitting in
> front of a narrow-minded preacher and next to lifeless
> faces?[33]

It is worth introducing two caveats at this point. In a nice
irony, Stark and Finke point out that the same modern marginalization of the Church that leads to numerical decline
also creates competitive conditions among newer expressions
of Church, with the more successful competitors experiencing
growth.[34] Indeed, such competition is necessary for sustain-
ing intensity of commitment under present Western conditions. As Charles Taylor observes, "Only small, committed
minorities, battling with their surroundings, have been able to

maintain 100 percent commitment by 100 percent of members."[35] So, an environment in which the Church is margin-
alized, with choosing and instrumental rationality redefining
religious attachment, need not mean that all the numbers will
trend downward. Global South-influenced and other Pentecostal churches are growing in parts of the West, after all,
despite overall Church involvement declining.

A second caveat is introduced by Robert Bellah as he
reflects on Church involvement in these newer Western conditions, where a premium is placed on expressive individualism. His point is meant to be positive and reassuring. He
reflects that today's primary language, at home with exploring and expressing personal needs, lacks the capacity to articulate anything deeper or more objective. This is because our
more expressive culture transmutes normative commitments
into various self-fulfillment options.[36] But Bellah is confident that a second language is present behind the primary
one, even though it cannot normally be given voice—that
there are hidden depths remaining below the surface.

This recalls how regular churchgoers have characteristically described what the Church means to them. It consoles
and reassures them. They find the music uplifting. They say
that a service was enjoyable. Or that they really value the
community involvement. In such cases, there can be more
going on than is readily expressible. But it is not easy in our
culture to describe music without focussing on how it makes
you feel, or uplifting worship without just talking about feel-
ing uplifted.

Yet is it the case that behind the language of uplift and
reassurance experienced in worship there is something more
that is straining toward expression—something like, "in word
and sacrament we meet Jesus Christ"? Sometimes this is no
doubt the case, though surely not always. Bellah enjoins a
measure of care so that we do not underestimate unplumbed

depths of faith and commitment that may be present despite appearances. However, while acknowledging his quite proper concern, I would urge an equal measure of care about overestimating those depths.

Indifference or hostility toward the Church, which is widespread in the West, along with spasmodic attendance and even nonattendance among avowed Christians, leads us to query what second language about the Church dimension of Christianity might be present. It could be that Taylor's "cross pressure" of belief and unbelief is at work, with some sort of Christian claim being registered though without any accompanying need to give it public expression—and this might represent a sense of decent spiritual reserve rather than simply diffidence. Or it may be read less positively. The second language here could be expressing a common Reformation-era claim that there is an invisible Church of the elect that is purer and truer than the corrupt, visible Church, which justifies avoiding the latter. If so, here is a further marginalization of the actual Church among those who might still assert their Christianity while not attending worship. In a scene from the now-classic streaming series *Mad Men*, set in the Drapers' kitchen in the New York suburbs, young daughter Sally asks her mother why their Black maid goes to Church every Sunday while they do not, to which Betty Draper tellingly replies, "We don't need to."

Charles Taylor refers to "stadial consciousness," meaning the irreversibility of these cultural transformations, which blocks any return of the Church's lost cultural and cosmological pre-eminence. He declares that there is a ratchet at the end of Western modernity's shift to a human-centered world.[37] In consequence, Church involvement cannot now be anything other than a matter of choosing. Likewise, we must acknowledge and work with the shift away from a hardware mentality to a software one—that the Western Church is now more likely to be seen as a provider of resources than a place of unconditional abiding. And besides, all that settled abiding came to be experienced by many modern Westerners as oppressive and confining rather than integrative and reassuring.

If we cannot return uncritically to a place of settled abiding, however, it does not follow that we must settle for permanent spiritual drift and unresolvedness. As Wuthnow reflects, "If spirituality once provided people with a sacred home, they do not simply abandon the quest for such a home *but rethink what a home may mean* now that they feel spiritually homeless."[38] So, what if there is a third way that leads to a new appreciation of Church, beyond what we have seen so far? This is what I will be considering in what follows. In any event, we cannot seek to ignore this modern turn to the subject, as Roger Haight insists, without failing to communicate with a whole culture.[39]

For Reflection and Discussion

- What is good and bad about our secular age?

- Which comes first, the Church or the Christian?

- What do you make of the young Dietrich Bonhoeffer's maxim, "a Christian who stays away from the assembly is a contradiction in terms"?

- What does the Church's Liturgical Year mean to you?

CHAPTER

3

Abiding in the Vine

I am the vine, you are the branches. Those who abide in me and I in them bear much fruit, because apart from me you can do nothing.

John 15:5

Christianity is not a religion; it is a Church.

G.K. Chesterton
Where All Roads Lead, 52

O
f the two epigraphs that begin this chapter, the second is intentionally provocative, though the first is scarcely less so. John's Jesus, who takes upon himself the divine self-designation "I am" from Exodus 3:14, goes on to declare an integral oneness with his followers. They are not branches attached to Jesus as if he were *the stem*, however. Instead, as potentially detachable branches they nevertheless share in who Jesus is *as the whole vine*, apart from which they can have no meaningful let alone effective Christian identity.

Here we are in tune with St Paul, from 1 Corinthians 12:12–27 and Romans 12:4–5, with his defining image of the Church as Christ's body, so that Christians should regard themselves as no less than conjoint body parts. As Dietrich Bonhoeffer sums it up, "The New Testament knows a form of revelation, 'Christ existing as church-community'."[1] In the subsequent school of Paul, the imagery develops. Christ's body on the cross serves to reconcile his body the Church (Ephesians 2:15), of which Christ is the head (Colossians 1:18), whose Easter triumph resounding through the whole cosmos is also the Church's triumph: "And [God the Father] has put all things under his feet and has made him the head over all things for the church, which is his body, the fullness of him who fills all in all" (Ephesians 1:22–23). So, the Church shares intimately and necessarily in who Christ now is as Lord of the cosmos. In exploring this theme, I will use the image of our heart's double beat: the systolic inflow and diastolic outflow.

The Systole

If you are looking for a more mystical version of Christianity, you would be hard pressed to improve on this New Testament conviction: that Christ is alive in his Church, and that the Church abides in Christ's ongoing life, compared with merely following his ethical teachings or seeking "inspiration for living" (alongside other potential sources). This is mystical, and it is frankly specific—although, almost paradoxically, it is also supremely inclusive given what is universally on offer. So, when that Catholic provocateur G.K. Chesterton spurned modern humanity's autonomous religious (and spiritual) quest in favor of designating Christianity simply and entirely as a Church, he was being mystical as well as provocative, while also quite scriptural. More than any kind of message or belief, then— let alone a take-it-or-leave-it one—Christianity is essentially a fellowship, a movement, a body. The Church follows the logic of the incarnate Word as the necessary embodiment of all things Christian.

It is normal today, however, for reasons aired in Chapter 2, to consider Christianity as only circumstantially related to the Church. Spiritual and personal resourcing is displacing ecclesial belonging. That state is now understood if at all to be a matter of choice, and Church involvement need not register as particularly significant in assessing someone's spiritual or even their Christian condition. In this individualistic reduction, religious institutions become merely potentially useful constructs for helping individuals along whichever spiritual path they might choose.

But these widely accepted rules of association are not sufficient to account for the Church *theologically*—that is, from the perspective of God's nature and purposes made manifest in Jesus Christ. For Dietrich Bonhoeffer, neither generic religiousness nor individualistic impulse nor the fact that humans need each other, nor any purely sociological explanation, can adequately account for the Church, because "in no [such] case is the starting point sought by acknowledging the reality of God's church-community as a revealed reality. And so, it is certain from the outset that the concept of the church will not be reached."[2] But the New Testament and the early Church start with the theological reality, and hence tell a different story.

Accordingly, the Church is neither a federation of congregations, nor at the congregational level is "she" a gathering of individuals who have embraced the Christian faith nor, for de Lubac, "is she an external organism brought into being or adopted after the event by the community of believers."[3] Closer to hardware, then, than to software. In similar Catholic vein another Cardinal, Walter Kasper, declares that "The communion of the church does not come about 'from below': it is grace and gift, common participation in the one truth, in the one life, and in the one love which God communicated to us in word and sacrament through Jesus Christ, in the Holy Spirit."[4]

Instead of a message, then, there is a communion. Instead of Christian individuals making the Church, as followers of an individual Christ, the Church *is* Christ in thoroughly relational form, and from that reality the Church makes Christian individuals. Indeed, it makes them to be more than individuals: *persons*, that is, who are more connected and rounded in their nature than are autonomous individuals. This is a point made radically by Bonhoeffer, who saw individuality as at best preliminary and undeveloped—as only a stage on the way to fuller personhood in what he called the Church community.[5] Christians are invited to discover the truth of Jesus Christ from the inside and thus to become their truly personal selves, which is the gift and calling of baptism.

The Holy Trinity, which situates Christ alive and active in the Holy Spirit at the heart of divine mystery, can be seen as God's revealed template for the Church, which is in turn a relational mystery participating in the oneness of Trinitarian life.[6] And from that divine *systole* comes the Church's missional *diastole*: its sacramental participation in the Holy Trinity's own relationality, or at least its aptness for it, grounds its witness and mission to a confused and violent world. This points beyond what philosophical and socio-political systems have struggled to accomplish in an increasingly nihilistic West.[7]

In making this claim, it is important to be clear about what is not being said. The Church is not just about doing and acting. In some contexts—and widely so within English and Australian Anglicanism—the buzzword is mission.[8] Yet while mission language in the Church is essential, as the use of fire is also essential, it can do damage if we are not careful. The great Swiss Protestant theologian Emil Brunner famously wrote that "The Church exists by mission, just as a fire exists by burning. Where there is no mission there is no Church; and where there is neither Church nor mission, there is no faith."[9] But this is only a half-truth.

The Church is a sacramental participation in the joy and the relationality of God, from which mission flows naturally as diastole follows systole. However, to emphasize mission apart from the context of sacramental, Trinitarian abiding is to risk putting the cart before the horse, not to mention laying a great and unrelieved burden on Christians who actually have to carry out that mission. I thoroughly endorse Brunner's refusal to separate Church from Christian faith—that is the point of this book—and I further affirm that mission is integral to the Church's proper identity. But here Brunner provides only half the story. Identifying the Church tautologously with missional activity is surely neither exclusively nor exhaustively true. One could equally say that the Church exists by abiding in the vine as breathing exists by respiration. So, while mission is an imperative for the Church it does not *make* the Church. We can likewise affirm that the Church exists by Eucharistic joy, by loving fellowship, by abiding in the Christian narrative, by Trinitarian participation.

But neither is the Church just about being, as if that can or should be separated from acting—from mission. My image of the heart, in which the systolic inflow of blood beats rhythmically with its diastolic outflow, captures the necessary order of gift and task (Karl Barth), of overture and reception, of contemplation and action, of prayer and work—the Benedictine *ora et labora*—and, paradigmatically, of Mary's hugely consequential "yes" to the divine Annunciation (Luke 1:38). Christ works through the Holy Spirit in the Church's work, by systole and diastole.

So, while we properly talk about the Church's function, the Church must not be understood functionally. There is often a sad and self-justifying busyness about Christianity in today's West, displayed in a widespread desire to be *relevant*, to be helpful (or, worse still, to be *useful*)—to be doing something worthwhile. Which is to wrongly suggest that abiding in the love and life of God through Christ in word and sacrament, and soaking in the Christian narrative like a restorative bath, is not also of the essence. Without an evident joy in the faith and practice of Christianity made manifest in the quality of Christian life and fellowship, no one is likely to be persuaded and want to join, and neither is a world full of well-intentioned agencies likely to sense anything distinctive about the Church.

The joy of saints and martyrs shows that there is more to the Church's doing and acting than right-mindedness and good intentions, which lack the surprise value of the divine systole and the un-self-regarding release of the divine diastole. The American Orthodox theologian Alexander Schmemann warned the Church about forgetting this joy and gift, which lies at the heart of Eastern Orthodox liturgy. He enjoins us to recover the Church's priestly calling to celebrate the world's creation and re-creation through Jesus Christ, in place of casting about for relevance like any other well-intentioned secular agency.[10] Ideally, then, the Eucharistic joy of Sunday converts the working week that follows, while the quiet joy insinuating itself through lives marked by *ora* helps to guide, transform, and empower their subsequent *labora*.

I now want to turn to that *labora* and consider God's deep purposes for the Church, while continuing to ensure that nothing functional is being commended that is not first rooted in the substantive—the diastolic recognized as reliant upon while also inseparable from the systolic.

The Diastole

God's deep purposes are revealed for Christians in the life, ministry, death, resurrection, and ascension of Jesus Christ, whose continuing presence is articulated using Holy Spirit language. It was the Church that told Jesus's story, beginning with the letters of Paul that witnessed to Jesus's impact and then the Gospels with their crafted narratives of his life. So, Jesus makes the Church, but it is the Church that makes Jesus known. Indeed, as Walter Kasper points out, "Without the church and its testimony we should know nothing of Jesus Christ. Without the church there would be no Holy Scripture. Scripture came into being in the church and for the church."[11]

The deep purpose of God for the Church is thus inseparable from Jesus, the head of the body, and his making flesh of God's nature and purposes. That purpose is to lift human beings up into God's life and hence into the truth of their own lives, caught up in Jesus Christ then sent out to share what they have found. This is what salvation means, through a community planted in the world to show what salvation looks like.[12] It brings the transformation of individuals, wider communities, and the world. This is the Church's proper action and mission, rooted in its truest being and nature. It embodies and celebrates as well as announces a new beginning for humanity in Jesus Christ.

In a paradigmatic scriptural testimony to this new beginning, Pentecost reverses the division of prideful humanity as it was imagined in the tower of Babel legend (Genesis 11:1–9), with its punishing divine imposition of mutually exclusive languages. In the upper room at Pentecost, however, a polyglot humanity finds itself singing from the same hymn sheet in praise of Jesus Christ (Acts 2:1–11), as the Holy Spirit makes the Church a sign and foretaste of God's plan for a reconciled humanity. And this world-transforming outcome is not just wishful thinking. As the English Evangelical theologian Graham Tomlin points out, "the hard evidence that God will one day bring all things together under Christ is found in all these small Christian communities scattered around the Roman Empire, which are busy uniting Gentile and Jew, free people and slaves, women and men."[13]

Indeed, there is no substitute for such witness. The missionary Bishop Lesslie Newbigin insisted that nothing less than a visible demonstration of this new reality would do to confirm it and win over adherents, declaring the faithful Christian congregation to be essential for showing what Jesus Christ means. He asks, "How is it possible that the gospel should be credible, that people should come to believe that the power which has the last word in human affairs is represented by a man hanging on a cross?" For Newbigin, "the only answer, *the only hermeneutic of the gospel*, is a congregation of men and women who believe it and live by it."[14] Of course, we must also acknowledge a wider range of Christian witness, including bishops, theologians, and saints along with members and leaders of the congregation, though the congregation celebrating word and sacrament is typically the place where Christian identity is encountered and formed.

In a book entitled *Does God Need the Church?*, German Catholic New Testament scholar Gerhard Lohfink answers the question posed by his book's title with a "yes," *if* God's purposes entail the enactment of salvation within the fabric of human life and history. In that case, such a divine commitment to humanity necessarily had to begin somewhere with a visible and tangible expression of the salvation that God intended.[15] That beginning was the election of Israel, which was declared, unpacked, and variously expressed in the Hebrew Scriptures/ Old Testament. And it was from this unrevoked calling of Israel that the Church emerged with Jesus the Jew, standing alongside Israel and universalizing its mission.

There is nothing self-aggrandizing about being God's chosen people, however, as Jews ancient and modern can tragically testify. "Israel's being chosen is not a privilege or a preference *over others*," says Lohfink, "but existence *for others*, and hence the heaviest burden in history."[16] And what Lohfink says of Israel also applies to the Church.

> The concept crystallizes Israel's knowledge that God desires to liberate and change the entire world but for that purpose needs a beginning in the midst of the world, as visible place and living witnesses. This has not the slightest thing to do with preference, advantage, elitism, or being better than, but it has a great

deal to do with God's respect for human dignity and freedom.[17]

Abiding in the Vine in Today's West: Dwelling and Seeking

God's calling of a people to abide in and then to share a world-transforming love is a demanding one. This is especially the case under present conditions in the West, where the Church has lost or is fast losing its former standing.

But behind the challenges facing today's Church in the West, a number of which we have considered, lies a divine invitation. There have been many defining moments in Church history, and this is a further one—a *kairos*, to use the New Testament term: a moment in time when God is bringing something new to birth.[18] We could do worse than describe the Western Church as now having to undergo a transition from *dwelling* to *seeking*, as expressed by Robert Wuthnow.[19] He is referring to a change in attitudes toward congregational belonging from the 1950s onward. But we can read this distinction more broadly as a departure from the givens of Christendom—of collective abiding in a settled world of meaning based on Christian beliefs, deeply-rooted practices, and their cosmic presuppositions—to embrace a new way of being Christian, as individuals seek meaning and purpose with a deeper appreciation of what belonging to the Church means. For many, this manifests the newer software mentality, as discussed in the last chapter. They are spiritual seekers who may or may not call themselves Christians but who look to the Church for resources as and if required. And indeed, spiritual seekers are also well represented among those who are entirely committed to the Church. With the best will in the world, even serious Christians in today's West no longer find themselves uncomplicatedly dwelling. They too are now seekers, albeit seekers after a greater fullness of life in Christ, in what is becoming a seeking Church.

So, we are at a *kairos* moment, a "God moment," in which the Church is being invited to reimagine what abiding in the vine can mean. It is a maturing opportunity, and like all such opportunities it can bring discomfort along with new insight. Here, the Church is called to share the restlessness of our times and the deep challenges to a settled sense of God's reassuring presence that modern horrors have brought, along with a troubling mood of ennui and anomie that afflicts today's young and old alike. This adds up to a sense of God's hiddenness, which has been a mainstay of modern literature[20] (think of Dostoyevsky's *The Brothers Karamazov* and Eliot's "The Wasteland"). A version of Church that offers easy comforts—which frowns on preaching that too serious-mindedly both engages and challenges modern preoccupations, preferring to avoid such involvement—is widely favored, but clinging to such avoidant comforts will not help to recapture yesterday's mood of dwelling. Even the unquiet conservatives in Western churches, who typically resist this transition, are in fact making this transition—though badly. We have all become seekers, but what many of the Church's conservatives are seeking is an escapist turning back of the clock.

The alternative is to recognize that God's people should not expect to find—and, according to scripture's witness, never have found—an easy settledness. There is a proper restlessness involved in God's calling of a people, which the English theologian John Macquarrie declares to be a defining characteristic.[21] This restlessness may have been less evident looking back on the Christendom era, when Christianity enjoyed cultural hegemony. But unsettled restlessness certainly marked the people of God according to Genesis and Exodus, with constant forward movement in pursuit of God's promise of a place to dwell. Nor should Christians reading the New Testament be left in any doubt that this applies to them, too: "For here we have no lasting city, but we are looking for the city that is to come" (Hebrews 13:14).

Yet, equally, the seeker must not despise the prospect of eventually coming to dwell. It is hard to imagine that the spiritual quest, which may have been experienced in somewhat dramatic terms, might eventually lead to Sunday-by-Sunday worship in a plain Christian fellowship of word and sacrament, perhaps in that church on the corner. There is a humility in accepting such an outcome that will elude the wrongly motivated seeker, as we see with Naaman the Syrian, who resented the undramatic ordinariness of Elisha the Prophet's proposed remedy for his disfigurement (2 Kings 5:9–14). Yet it does happen, and you will kindly indulge me if I give an example. Two serious, long-term students and practitioners of Eastern spiritual wisdom found their way to the little Anglican congregation where I served and to its weekly Eucharist—and indeed, that church is actually on their corner—because they had the wit and grace to see seeking and dwelling as compatible. Who would have thought that Eastern meditation and yoga might find their way to baptism and confirmation? But this is one way that abiding in the vine will manifest itself in our day.

Robert Wuthnow points to a key instance in Western Christian tradition where dwelling and seeking are mutually informing. He refers to

the sixth-century Rule of Saint Benedict, which asks monks to take vows of stability, *conversatio*, and obedience. Stability emphasizes settledness; *conversatio* change; and obedience suggests a need for commitment to both.... *Conversatio* is a commitment to live faithfully in unsettled times and to keep one's life sufficiently unsettled to respond to the changing voice of

> God. . . . The wisdom of Saint Benedict is that dwell-
> ing and seeking are both part of what it means to be
> human.[22]

Here we see that a properly settled sense of abiding does not
just fall into the lap of Christians. The Church is on pilgrimage to the heavenly city through the earthly one, which is a
journey of discovery, conversion, and purgation. Humbly following the shamed and crucified Jesus Christ requires honest
self-assessment from the Church, with a refusal to settle for
superficial comforts in some half-converted way station. This
is the purpose of the Church's Lenten season with its annually
repeated challenge. One might say, then, that seeking is properly part of abiding, or dwelling, in the vine—indeed, abiding
is a gift that must be grown into, which is a matter of seeking
and never settling for some illusory homecoming.

God unsettles the settled, then, but with a view to seeing
them truly settled. The Exodus journey of God's first people to the promised land was tortuous, but all their seeking
took place while dwelling in God's promise—even though it
remained a promise for forty years. Likewise, today's seekers
are not meant to drift forever, destined to be aimless wander-
ers. The pilgrim journey has its proper ending, and a Church
of seeking must also be the Church of finding. Indeed, as
Wuthnow warns, there is no effective spiritual seeking that
does not entail some abiding. "A spirituality of seeking," he
writes, "is invariably too fluid to provide individuals with the
social support they need or to encourage the stability and
dedication required to grow spiritually and to mature in char-
acter. It was not without reason that the Rule of Saint Benedict emphasized obedience rather than stability or *conversatio*
alone."[23]

We have been considering the systole and then the diastole, with God's purposes grounded in and emerging from

the Church's abiding in the vine. That abiding for the Church in today's West cannot simply be a matter of untroubled dwelling, however, but it properly involves the seeking that has always been a mark of God's people on pilgrimage. This extended from the Genesis journeys of the patriarchs and Israel's wilderness wanderings following the Exodus to the settled abiding of Benedictine monasteries that were at the same time engines of spiritual maturation (along with significant agrarian and socio-economic transformation in medieval Europe), embracing a stability that was never meant to get too comfortable (hence the stricter Cistercian evolution of Benedictine life from the late-eleventh century). With these considerations in mind and the horse firmly before the cart, I now want to set out what I regard to be the Church's key mission in today's West. It is to discover and to model and witness a genuine abiding together in peace.

The Nontribal Tribe

I have discussed the individualism that is transforming not only the cultural but also the ecclesial landscape in today's West. I suggested that a shift from individual to person is the preferred Christian outcome—that is, from a two- to a three-dimensional, properly relational existence, beyond the delusions of autonomy.

The individual in today's West is, after all, a threatened and unstable creature. As Christopher Lasch unsparingly regarded it, in *The Minimal Self*, the Western individual is a narcissistic survivalist characterized by a loss of hope and a weak, undefined sense of self, withdrawn into a world of image rather than reality, and unable to adequately distinguish self from others (think of Narcissus). Like Freud, he wants to strengthen the ego, but how does one do that? And the problem is only getting worse, as we have seen over the forty years since Lasch's book came out. The rise of identity politics in the West represents an attempt to strengthen the self as contesting alternatives proliferate, but is it working? One could argue that things are made worse by the rivalry and hostility that accompany today's constant defining, redefining, policing, and questioning of identity. This has become a central feature of life in the Anglosphere, thanks in part to America's increasingly virulent culture wars and their export.

But what if the individual is better understood as a node in a network of mutual influence, rather than a stand-alone center of more-or-less stable identity? I maintain that the individual and the community are woven fine, representing different aspects of the one human reality. We are deeply, chronically interdependent and mutually invested, for good or ill, and the interwoven pathologies of both individual and communal existence are everywhere on display. Yet so are the hopefulness and creativity that we evoke in one another. The Church reflects both, being fully immersed in the world and its problems while also being called to become a sign of healing for the nations (Revelation 22:2).

In today's environment of worsening, self-defining rivalries, individuals are swept up into mutually exclusive groups with competing narratives. Daily, we see every cool-headed claim to objectivity and common-sense realism being trashed as authoritarian populists and their sycophants seek to build a new post-democratic order based on lies and the hyping of grievance. Healthy democracy calls for a secure sense of self along with an underlying measure of solidarity, which together make robust yet civilized debate possible, but all of that is increasingly inconceivable. In this context, churches are readily enlisted in the culture wars, as we see with Putin's anti-Western and only nominally Orthodox Christian fever dream of a renewed Russian empire—also with the rancid Christian nationalist far-right in the land of Trump, his craven acolytes, and his imitators. In the latter case, we observe what one journalist has felicitously called "a party's self-perpetuation for its own sake driven by an opportunistic indifference to fact and reason, expressed through coarse and incendiary rhetoric,"[24] yet Christian churches and their leaders are prepared to give this travesty their blessing.

The Church has to be a tribe—it will be identifiable in the midst of other tribes, with its own cultures, rules, and terminology. *But does it have to be tribal or tribalistic?* Might a world of hostile tribes benefit from there being at least one tribe that approaches distinctiveness and difference differently—*a non-tribal tribe?*[25]

The Church was born as a very particular body according to the Pentecost narrative, yet a radically inclusive one. And this inclusivity is based not on Enlightenment tolerance, which readily slides into mutual indifference, but on God's dream for humanity. According to that Pentecost narrative (Acts 2:1–11) the Holy Spirit took a tour around all those named parts of the Empire to gather a great diversity together in unity. Those present were Jews and converts to Judaism, but the extension of Israel's promise to the Gentiles through Jesus Christ makes the point even more strikingly. The great text is Ephesians 2:11–22, where the dividing wall of hostility is broken down between Jew and Gentile, radically expanding the scope of God's chosen people. In the NRSV, it reads:

> So then, remember that at one time you Gentiles by birth, called "the uncircumcision" by those who are called "the circumcision"—a physical circumcision made in the flesh by human hands—remember that you were at that time without Christ, being aliens from the commonwealth of Israel, and strangers to the covenants of promise, having no hope and without

God in the world. But now in Christ Jesus you who once were far off have been brought near by the blood of Christ. For he is our peace; in his flesh he has made both groups into one and has broken down the dividing wall, that is, the hostility between us. He has abolished the law with its commandments and ordinances, that he might create in himself one new humanity in place of the two, thus making peace, and might reconcile both groups to God in one body through the cross, thus putting to death that hostility through it. So he came and proclaimed peace to you who were far off and peace to those who were near; for through him both of us have access in one Spirit to the Father. So then you are no longer strangers and aliens, but you are citizens with the saints and also members of the household of God, built upon the foundation of the apostles and prophets, with Christ Jesus himself as the cornerstone. In him the whole structure is joined together and grows into a holy temple in the Lord; in whom you also are built together spiritually into a dwelling place for God.

It is remarkable that any Christian could read let alone dwell on this passage and then be able to engage in faith-based rivalry and even violence in a thoroughly tribal way. Because here is a template for difference that does not entail tribalistic division—a difference that does not have to be weaponized against the other in defence of the same. Here is a comprehensive charity and graciousness that does not come from conventional morality but from God's gift in Jesus Christ, which is implanted in a world that is not otherwise capable of such a breakthrough. Here is the renewed sociality that restores humanity to its created vocation of living in unity and peace.[26] For Australian Anglican theologian

Stephen Pickard, "the Church is that form of life that makes explicit what is true about the world created and loved by God."[27]

The death of Jesus Christ has prompted many Christians to see violence and suffering as somehow holy and to seek revenge, as in the antisemitism that is making a return with authoritarian populism. But the truth of Easter is that the worst of violent human self-preservation and self-aggrandisement—collective, tribal realities that march in time with individual weakness and its pathologies—is borne personally by God on Good Friday and turned inside out on Easter Sunday. Which means forgiveness not payback, transformation not damnation, and hope rather than a life stitched together out of despair.

It means empowerment to become a different type of human entity, individually because collectively—a nontribal tribe. And a nonreligious religion, too, if religion is the sociological name for what binds a tribal group together. We see religion functioning positively in this way, yes, but so often negatively when it baptizes hatred and division. Secularization helps Christianity here, enabling it to become what French social scientist Marcel Gauchet calls the religion of the exit from religion.[28]

If all this is true, then the Church should be able to stand at the forefront of healing and transformation in the world. And, again, not because tolerance and welcome are widely praised virtues in today's West, but because before all that, a deep and otherwise unreachable current of longsuffering and welcome was unleashed in the world. This is the ongoing work of Jesus Christ through the Holy Spirit. Here the deep purposes of God are entrusted to the institution that is called to abide in the vine that is Jesus Christ—to inhabit its birthright, as God's perennial challenge to the errant powers and principalities that otherwise threaten to define and debauch reality. This is the foundational Christian mission: "to bring to the gentiles the news of the boundless riches of Christ and to make everyone see what is the plan of the mystery hidden for ages in God, who created all things, so that through the church the wisdom of God in its rich variety might now be made known to the rulers and authorities in the heavenly places" (Ephesians 3:8b–10).

Many examples could be given of the increasingly tribalistic context in which the nontribal tribe must make its stand, but I will confine myself to what is currently the most incendiary of these. Lasch believed that paranoia was becoming a substitute for religion in the West because it proposes a hidden principle at work behind surface appearances.[29] I read this as a particular instance of what is now emerging as a major new Western phenomenon, as public discourse is increasingly hijacked by perpetually scandalized conspiracy theorists who are seemingly inured to reality. This angry self-definition by affronted minorities makes an identity out of genuine or else strategically confected grievance, then weaponizes that grievance in hatred of the demonized other.

Over the last century, we have seen fascist and communist excesses of this phenomenon, most notably in the form of race hatred. A supposedly threatened group accustomed to some measure of prosperity, privilege, and power turns on a weaker group—one which it has been conditioned by propaganda to regard as a looming threat. Many on the American far right have been steered into resentment of black and brown people because whites will soon be a minority in America—a simple piece of demographic inevitability that is whipped up into a covert left-wing conspiracy of intentional race replacement. Here is the Ku Klux Klan mentality, though with the lynching and burning only currently appearing in small doses (e.g., in America there is the typical death row racial demographic, excessive police violence against African Americans, the Capitol insurrection, and the growing resistance to historical truth-telling about racial injustice).[30]

All this is made worse by the twin menaces of "angertainment" on the right-wing fringes of traditional curated media along with the algorithm-driven social media platforms that electronically magnify disinformation and hatred. These have fueled shocking mimetic violence in countries as diverse as Sri Lanka, Myanmar, Brazil, and the United States. Here we see the emergence of what amounts to an alternative church, knit together with a powerful and appealing narrative, replete with heroes and villains, apocalyptic warnings about the coming obliteration of an already-vanishing way of life, and a call for heroic sacrifice from that alternative church's "true believers," who may be required to stand up and do something—as they did on January 6, 2021 in Washington.

The algorithms that steer social media searches and direct users to new webpages favor connections that maximize time on the site, and hence potential advertising revenue, so it is in the interest of these businesses to keep users glued to the screen, giving them more and more of their favored content to fixate on.[31] Contrary to how this is presented by its promoters, social media is not primarily about authentic selves soberly in search of information, resources, and benign connections. Instead, it is an engine of obsession and rivalry, functionally religious, and a vector of violent contagion.

There is a different air to breathe once that dividing wall of hostility named in Ephesians 2:14 is broken down: a nonadversarial air. It is the infusion of an at-homeness with God, an abiding in the vine. It means that in today's unsettled West, it remains possible simply to be calm and to breathe. Of course, there will be challenges and struggles for the Church in these new conditions, but these will be the right sort of challenges and struggles: to enter more fully into our spiritual inheritance in Christ, which is at the same time to be enlisted in the service of God's historical purposes. And this is as true for Christian individuals as it is true for the Church.

Evoking a great yet widely untapped spiritual current in Catholic tradition, Gerard Manley Hopkins describes this new atmosphere that we can breathe as Marian air. The grace and beauty of Mary's openness to God in the Annunciation help to secure the Church's and the Christian's sense of abiding in Christ and to enable our extension of that world-healing capacity:

> Stir in my ears, speak there
> Of God's love, O live air,
> Of patience, penance, prayer:
> World-mothering air, air wild,
> Wound with thee, in thee isled,
> Fold home, fast fold thy child.[32]

Of course, the Church falls short of its vision splendid—and often spectacularly, even programmatically. So, it will not do to be too idealistic about the Church, which is a recipe for discouragement, bitterness, and scandal on the part of those whom the Church has failed or betrayed. But neither can we forget scriptural and credal assurances. The patience of God and the solidarity of the crucified Christ remain with a stumbling and often recalcitrant Church. What else, when all is said and done, does the Church have to rely on but Christ's promise: "And remember, I am with you always, to the end of the age" (Matthew 28:20)? I will keep this hope in mind in the next chapter, where I address the Church's faults as frankly and nondefensively as I can. It is indeed into earthen vessels—into clay pots—that God's treasure has been placed.

For Reflection and Discussion

- Is the best argument for Christianity a faithful congregation?

- Does God need the Church? Why so?

- What does salvation look like?

- As a Christian, are you "seeking," "dwelling," or both?

CHAPTER

4

Treasure
in Earthen Vessels

But we have this treasure in earthen vessels, to show that the transcendent power belongs to God and not to us.

2 Corinthians 4:7

Jesus's followers can be terrible. They can screw up, they can hurt and maim, and they can be the reason why people lose their faith altogether. . . . The cold, hard truth, the wretched truth of the matter, is that the opposite is also true.

Martha Tatarnic
Why Gather? The Hope and Promise of the Church, 40

Yet saints their watch are keeping,
their cry goes up, "How long?"

Samuel John Stone
from "The Church's One Foundation"

I t will not do to pretend that all is well with the Church. To more-or-less glibly deny the seriousness of the Church's failings, refusing the hard work of honest institutional self-examination and conversion, is to further ignore and disrespect those whom the Church has wronged. The obvious reference here is to the treachery represented by clergy sexual abuse, not only of young children but also of teenagers and vulnerable adults. Victims have had their futures ruined, their mental health and relationship prospects undermined, their faith betrayed and stolen, and in many tragic instances, they have been driven to death by suicide. What is more, churches have refused to face these grievous wrongs and to take collective responsibility, as if an abusive cleric can be sufficiently understood as a lone predator rather than the manifestation of a dysfunctional church-family system that they arguably are.[1]

Another current issue has to do with sexuality and gender. Women still have to make their way in churches that either refuse outright or at least struggle to treat them as equal and to take their aspirations seriously. Likewise, LGBTQIA+ people look to the Church for bread and are too often given a stone (Matthew 7:9). This is the case among both Catholics and Evangelicals, with strange bedfellows of both sensibilities within the Anglican GAFCON[2] movement prepared to split the Anglican Communion rather than compromise their hard line.

There is a widespread perception among the Church's critics that apprehensive, sexless perfectionism is the Christian ideal, nicely caught by William Blake's complaint that "Priests in black gowns were walking their rounds, And binding with briars, my joys & desires."[3] In light of this perception, which is not entirely unfounded, sexual abuse and its denial, also unease with the feminine and female sexuality, along with the rejection of homosexuality by churches that are afraid of it, can all be seen to manifest emotional immaturity, anxiety, and their pathologies. One recalls Jesus's warning, "Woe also to you lawyers! For you load people with burdens hard to bear, and you yourselves do not lift a finger to ease them" (Luke 11:46).

Then there are today's heretical distortions of Christianity evident in Russian and American so-called Christian Nationalism, and in the latter's alignment of Christianity with heavily armed white supremacism. The fact that churches provide a home for this and do not adequately call it out represents a further scandal. So, both within the Christian mainstream and on its fringes, churches engage in unchristian behavior while making unyielding demands that seem to deny the good news of Jesus Christ, who came to seek and save the lost (Luke 19:10). And it has ever been thus.

What are we to make of the Church and its claims if we are not prepared to overlook this compromised reality, which only a few current examples suffice to make plain? Do we give up on the Church, concluding that it is unreformable and irredeemable? Alternatively, do we seek to downplay the Church's problems? Do we offer too-easy assurances about the Church not really being like that, as if these problems are superficial or even coincidental? Or do we honestly face the music, though without letting it overwhelm us? Hence, St. Augustine's acknowledgement that the Church is perennially challenged by sinful members while it remains on track toward salvation thanks to God's mercy. How do we follow him in this double affirmation, continuing to say "yes" to the Church while admitting its errors, sins, and failures?

In this chapter, I will try to give a theological answer to this question without defining the Church's downside as purely sociological and hence separable from deeper theological considerations. Instead, let our theology of the Church be a theology of the actual church—not of some idealistic blueprint but of the Church's tangible reality, which is being crafted by God from the gnarled and crooked timber of human lives. Beyond ideals of perfectionism and purity, then, what is "that wonderful and sacred mystery"[4] of the Church, which continues to produce saints and keeps them resolutely on their watch? And how is that treasure to be found in such plainly earthen vessels?

Starting with the Actual Church

Instead of giving adequate weight to the Church's amoeba-like reality, indistinctness of witness and purpose, and its moral ambiguity, which makes it hard sometimes to adequately distinguish the Church's behavior from that of other worldly institutions,[5] the tendency in recent ecclesiology has been to seek a blueprint for the Church—for something normative, which is also something readily idealized.[6] But if we do that, according to Nicholas Healy, then

> The church's sinfulness can be considered as no more than a rather infrequent and finally insignificant distortion of the church's abiding fundamental reality, rather than an ever-present aspect of the Church's concrete identity. And this can lead to a naïve, complacent or worse attitude in those quarters of the church that subscribe to the view that "underneath" our visible flaws there lies the ideal heart of gold if only those carping critics had sufficient faith to see it.[7]

Yet surely such confidence in a truer, purer Church behind the actual, blemished, empirical one is cold comfort for the victim of sexual abuse, or for the woman demeaned by a Church that does not take her seriously, or for the committed gay Christian who hears that Pope Francis refuses to judge him though many in the Church still do, or even for the ordinary Christian or member of the clergy who has become accustomed to high-handed treatment from the congregation or the wider institutional Church. For all of these, their Christian faith may end up being in spite of the Church rather than because of it. Will they be reassured if told that the Church is not *really* like that?

St. Augustine set the Western direction in these matters by acknowledging the presence of clean and unclean in the Church until their separation at the final judgment. Many reprobates are caught up with the good in the gospel dragnet (Matthew 13:47–50), says Augustine, until that net is finally dragged to shore and the catch sorted. Here we recall Jesus's parable of the weeds sown among the wheat, with its refusal to have the weeds uprooted before harvest time in case the not-always-distinguishable young wheat might also be pulled up (Matthew 13:24–30). This sounds a warning against seeking a purer Church of the elect at the expense of God's actual Church, which is a cause in which fanatics have done much harm.[8] One reason to accept (if not to be entirely sanguine about) an imperfect Church is to consider the alternative, which typically involves zealous sectarianism.

But there are also benefits to be found in these circumstances for a Church whose mission is to demonstrate repentance and forgiveness rather than spiritual perfectionism, so that the Church's goodness remains godly and humane rather than the stuff of harsh enforcement and—let us be honest—often brittle pretense. We should not underestimate the theological value of the Church's struggles, then, which require us to live as disciples in a less than perfect institution.[9] As the Canadian Anglican priest and spiritual writer Martha Tatarnic says of the Church, "I need this mess of sin and blindness and fatal flaws in order to see for myself how grace really works, how love and forgiveness and redemption are real and powerful. Saying that Jesus is God is just an interesting thing to say, unless it has something to do with us. Not us as we wish we might be, or think we should be, but as we really are."[10]

For Augustine, the Church's state as a *corpus permixtum* presents it with a spiritual opportunity: "In this wicked world, and in these evil times, the Church through her present humiliation is preparing for future exaltation. She is being trained by the stings of fear, the tortures of sorrow, the distresses of hardship, and the dangers of temptation; and she rejoices only in expectation, when her joy is wholesome."[11] Indeed, Augustine sees Catholic faith being strengthened by its struggle with heretics and worldly philosophy, while the presence of sinners in its midst provides the Church with training in benevolence and endurance.[12] This was always Rowan Williams's approach as Archbishop of Canterbury, believing that we find the truth of God and our Christian selves in demanding encounters with difficult circumstances but especially with unassimilable others in the Church, refusing escapism in favor of persevering with the actual and the imperfect.[13]

Clearly, there is no idealizing of the Church going on here. It is bound for the heavenly city, while still part of the earthly city. Clearly, then, as Dietrich Bonhoeffer makes explicit, an act of faith is required to believe in the Church theologically given its present mixed state. Regrettably, however, many cannot attain or retain that faith considering what they have seen.

And what about the Church as a whole, rather than its individual members alone? Can the Church be wrong and sinful in and of itself? Many will say, "Of course it can, look at the institutional coverups." In reply, we will hear that these coverups represent just one more case of individual Christians acting in the wrong—in this case, certain bishops—rather than the whole Church being implicated. The Reformation-era Anglican answer to this question was not so squeamish, with a clear admission of error as a step on the way to necessary Church reform: "As the Church of Jerusalem, Alexandria, and Antioch, have erred; so also the Church of Rome hath erred, not only in their living and manner of Ceremonies, but also in matters of Faith."[14] This implies a denial in advance of the later doctrine of Papal Infallibility (1870), declared by Rome in the face of modern challenges to faith and Church authority.

One might argue that claiming infallibility for the Pope, even under the quite specific and hence limited conditions set down by the First Vatican Council,[15] makes the Roman Church more likely to resist soul-searching and refuse to admit its wrongs. This was argued by one of that Church's most critically loyal sons, the theologian Hans Küng. He was officially deprived of his *missio canonica* as a Catholic theologian in 1979 for listing his Church's historical and more recent erroneous claims, acknowledging the difficulties that these have caused for the faithful. Yet he still held to the Church's secure alignment with the truth because Jesus Christ remained present in it through his word and sacraments and will not let it stray too far from the truth.[16] There is a similarity here with Augustine's solution, to the extent that faith in the Church is solely reliant upon God's faithfulness in Jesus Christ. We can retain faith in the Church because God will vindicate it in the end (Augustine), while promising in the meantime to preserve it in the truth of Christ, though without preventing all error and wrongdoing (Küng).

Importantly, in neither case (St. Augustine and Hans Küng) do we have an invisible Church that is deemed to be separate from the actual, empirical, visible Church (a proposal associated with Clement of Alexandria). That would be to claim a supposedly truer, purer, deeper ecclesial reality, effectively untainted by stains on its surface. For Augustine, however, this distinction fared best when reframed as a dual perspective on the one, single, and only Church. The invisible Church thus becomes a way of talking about God's promise dwelling in the Church's visible, empirical reality. The invisible is more like the spiritual dimension of the visible, if you like, though these remain indivisible. It was later Reformed theology that defined and separated the invisible from the visible, denying that Rome was the true Church. As the Westminster Confession declared, "The catholic or universal church, which is invisible, consists of the whole number of the elect, that have been, are, or shall be gathered into one, under Christ the Head thereof . . . ."[17]

But this is not a sustainable New Testament distinction, as the Norwegian Lutheran theologian Harald Hegstad points out. At the beginning, there were simply communities of believers gathered around word and sacrament, which is what made each of them a fellowship in Jesus Christ. Moreover, the believers did not make the Church—these fellowships were not the source of Jesus's presence, but rather the result of it.[18] Jesus is not conjured up by pious believers, apart from which there is no Church; rather, the presence of Jesus in his word and sacraments makes the Church, which is then the mother of believers. Thus, Jesus's promise to abide with the Church forever (Matthew 28:20) becomes integral to defining the actual, empirical Church, of which it is the living spiritual principle. This represents Augustine's holding together of visible and invisible, with which Dietrich Bonhoeffer the Lutheran would certainly agree:

> We do not believe in an invisible church .... Instead we believe that God has made the concrete, empirical church ... in which the word is preached and the sacraments are celebrated to be God's own church-community .... We believe that it is the body of Christ, Christ's presence in the world, and that according to the promise God's Spirit is at work in it. ... We believe in the church not as an ideal that is unattainable or yet to be fulfilled, but as a present reality. Christian thinking, in contrast to all idealist theories of community, considers Christian community to be God's church-community at every moment in history. And yet within its historical development it never knows a state of fulfillment. It will remain impure as long as there is history, and yet this concrete form is nevertheless God's church-community.[19]

Walter Kasper, the German Catholic theologian, is also in agreement, arguing that the mystery of the Church is to be found in its exterior form and not anywhere in its interior—not, that is, in any fundamental visible/invisible distinction.[20] Here Kasper shares Augustine's conviction with the Lutherans, resting his faith in the Church on God's promise of faithfulness to Christ's bride and body.

All of this recalls traditional Catholic teaching on the validity of a sacrament: that Christ is reliably mediated through the Church's sacramental action, even if the one ministering it is unworthy by reason of sin. Recall, for example, Augustine's insistence against the schismatic fourth-century Donatists that those who abandoned the Church under persecution and later returned could still perform valid sacramental ministry. Such confidence relies on God's promise as a bridge across human failure and wrongdoing. This Catholic perspective found a Reformation-era Anglican echo in The Thirty-Nine Articles:

> Although in the visible Church the evil be ever mingled with the good, and sometimes the evil have chief authority in the Ministration of the Word and Sacraments, yet forasmuch as they do not the same in their own name, but in Christ's, and do minister by his commission and authority, we may use their Ministry, both in hearing the Word of God, and in receiving the Sacraments. Neither is the effect of Christ's ordinance taken away by their wickedness, nor the grace of God's gifts diminished from such as by faith, and rightly, do receive the Sacraments ministered unto them; which be effectual, because of Christ's institution and promise, although they be ministered by evil men.[21]

Likewise, the whole Church is not discredited, nor are its spiritual claims nullified, by the presence of sin within it. God's faithfulness must be weighed against human unfaithfulness.

To be sure, this reliance on God's promises may not satisfy the wronged or indeed sustain their faith in Christ once they have been betrayed. Though it does assure those who persevere in faith that the Church is still God's instrument—that the treasure remains in its earthen vessels. Believers must never treat this promise as a get-out-of-jail-free card, however, and let bad behavior become entrenched in the Church. In such cases, the promise has been occluded, and the gospel has not found its congregational hermeneutic.

Christ's Promise: Neither Perfection nor "Purity"

I have been suggesting that the Church is not an ideal entity constructed out of piety but something that God makes and sustains, in which there is room for sinners. There is no excuse, therefore, for loveless perfectionism and hard-edged impatience with other Christians, which represent a more subtly refined version of sin. Besides, the more perfect that others seem to us, the more reliably our rivalry and rancour can grow. A Christian fellowship aiming for sinless perfection is bound to disappoint, then, and often spectacularly. We see this whenever the fanatical sorting of wheat from chaff begins (Matthew 3:12), as in witch hunts, show trials, lynchings, and every other manifestation of humanity's hardwired recourse to scapegoating.[22] So, let there be renewing movements in the Church by all means, but let them not be driven by personal disappointments, grudges, and the violent hatred that these can spawn.

St. Paul's image of the Church as a body of conjoint members entails mutual nonrivalrous regard, which leads him to challenge Christian factionalism (1 Corinthians 3:1–9). Instead, he commends love in the Church with the hymn that includes 1 Corinthians 13:4–7. This text must not be confined to the wedding context where it is best known. Instead, it addresses the whole Church: "Love is patient; love is kind; love is not envious or boastful or arrogant or rude. It does not insist on its own way; it is not irritable or resentful; it does not rejoice in wrongdoing, but rejoices in the truth. It bears all things, believes all things, hopes all things, endures all things." Likewise, anger, cursing, and judgment within the Church are condemned by Jesus (Matthew 5:22). This is less about avoiding a moral wrong, however, and more about failing to adopt a God's-eye view of the Church's reality.

Such impatience with the actual Church in favor of some preferred version of it is something that Dietrich Bonhoeffer counseled against,[23] concerned as he was with disruptively radical reform movements (as was Luther) along with later pietistic sectarianism. "Genuine love for the church will bear and love its impurity and imperfection too," as Bonhoeffer writes, "for it is in fact this empirical church in whose womb grows God's sacred treasure, God's own church-community."[24]

To be sure, Bonhoeffer's love for the actual Church did not stop him from leaving official German Lutheranism for the new Confessing Church, protesting against the so-called German Christians and their collaboration with Nazism. But we remember that it was from the womb of ordinary German Protestantism, for Bonhoeffer and others like him, that the saints and martyrs of the Confessing Church emerged.

It is one thing to take an emergency step like that in fidelity to the gospel, however, and another to become a settled hater of fellow Christians. In fact, Bonhoeffer's breaking of fellowship can be read as an expression of love for the actual Church, inviting it to come to its senses. Teaching in Matthew's Gospel about handling intra-Church conflicts recommends such exclusion as the last resort in dealing with an invincibly intransigent church member: "If the member refuses to listen to them [i.e., to the complainant and one or two witnesses], tell it to the church; and if the offender refuses to listen even to the church, let such a one be to you as a Gentile and a tax collector" (Matthew 18:17). Yet we remember that Matthew himself was a tax collector—a hated collaborator with the occupying power— who had been welcomed and restored by Jesus, along with other tax collectors and sinners (Matthew 9:10–17, Mark 2:15– 22, Luke 5:29–39). So, Jesus's harsh-seeming instruction about breaking fellowship as a final expedient in Church discipline need not be read as permanent condemnation, but as a gesture that reveals the reality of already-broken fellowship and an invitation—albeit a tough-minded one—to be welcomed back with a changed attitude. For Bonhoeffer and the Confessing Church, then, their separation from the German Christians was also a wakeup call to those collaborators.

As for how to cope with the frustrations of sticking with a plainly imperfect Church, rather than leaving it, Peter Berger offers some theological guidance alongside some spiritual advice in the spirit of Bonhoeffer, whose position he was setting out:

> Psychologically speaking, one can explain one's adherence to the visible Christian assembly only in words similar to those one would use if asked why one loves one's mother. Only such love can overcome the many social scandalizations always present in the physical congregating of Christians, who remain what they are—Greeks, Jews, pietists, liberals, often concrete types that may be obnoxious and irritating—and yet, in the very act of assembling under God's word, become something else, something transfigured in Christ's presence. And the very particularities of those who sit side by side in such congregations is a reminder of God's will that we should love one another.[25]

Pastoral ministry is the abiding sign of God's patience with the Church, as priests and pastors labor to model and commend Christianity in churches and congregations that sometimes seem to be preferring something else. It is a spiritual challenge for priests and pastors to persevere in love, patiently bearing with many inevitable frustrations. In this task, they need the sustenance of scripture, which can be understood as God's love letter to reluctant people.

My personal challenge in this area was with what we might call Barbara Pym Anglicanism. According to its often-searing portrayals by that twentieth-century Jane Austen, the Anglican Church appears solely concerned with the reinforcement of social norms against a background of nominal Christianity, with little evidence that faith and the specifics of Christian belief have anything at all to do with it. Only intense sectarian churches can wholly escape this condition, though they face their own problems of intemperate zeal and judgmentalism. In both of these cases, it is chiefly patient and resilient pastoral ministry, which is loving and creative though not indulgent or sentimental, that represents God's embrace of the actual Church—the God who has not given up on Barbara Pym Anglicanism.

Purity is the problem here, which risks becoming a pathology akin to the unquiet condition of perfectionism. Yet we must be careful about overemphasizing purity if we are to remain faithful to scripture. We must not forget that the insistence on national purity found in Ezra and Nehemiah was undermined by the story of a Moabite foreigner in the Book of Ruth, who found her way into Jesus's own genealogy—indeed, she is the only mother mentioned in that whole exhaustive list apart from Mary, just to make sure that we do not miss the point (Matthew 1:5). Nor should we forget God's fidelity to his chosen but recalcitrant people as testified to in the story of Hosea the prophet and his wife of whoredom (Hosea 1:2–11), let alone throughout Israel's wilderness wanderings despite every provocation (Exodus 32:1–14). Likewise, Jesus associated with prostitutes, tax collectors, and other outsiders. Their place in the earliest Church communities along with slaves and all kinds of gentiles and foreigners reveals a radical message of inclusion with a disregard for maintaining conventional purity and its boundaries. This was also evident in Jesus's preferencing of people over the law—the spirit over the letter: 'Then he said to them, 'The Sabbath was made for humankind and not humankind for the Sabbath, so the Son of Man is lord even of the Sabbath'" (Mark 2:27–28).

This same Jesus, who gave communion at the Last Supper to Judas the traitor on the night of his betrayal and who presumably washed his feet, bears with his Church to the extent that his patience is absolutely of the essence. He contradicts the purist notion that fidelity to some truth must take precedence over fellowship in the Church. Instead, maintaining fellowship is what Jesus did. So, for us, it is the most evangelical thing to do and the truest path to Christlikeness.[26] The Episcopal theologian Ephraim Radner goes so far as to commend such patient and penitent abiding, even if the Church appears to be in ruins.[27]

In being prepared to draw near to and be counted with sinners in a sinful Church, we are drawing near to Christ in his self-emptying (*kenosis*),[28] along with his distinctive approach to sin through the cross and resurrection.[29] Jesus does not flinch from sin, although he has no part in it. And because of that sinlessness, he has nothing to prove—he has no superior status to secure over sinful others, which would be to play sin's game in an especially tiresome way. It would not make sense for the self-emptying Christ, poured out in solidarity with sinful humanity, to insist on being better than us. His love for us leaves no room for that. These claims are not only uncompromising, however, but they strike us as virtually inexplicable: "For our sake God made him to be sin who knew no sin, so that in him we might become the righteousness of God" (2 Corinthians 5:21). I recall a lector, who was preparing before the Eucharist to read a lectionary passage that contained this verse, coming into the sacristy to ask me if it was a misprint.

In his meditation on this theme, William Cavanaugh concludes that "A properly Chalcedonian Christology resists the Monophysite and Nestorian attempts to protect the divinity of Christ from contamination by sinful humanity. The drama of salvation lies entirely within the full assumption of our sinful humanity by Christ."[30] Jesus Christ so embraces the sinful human condition in patient, healing, reconciling love that it is as if he *becomes sin*, which is not to say that he gives in to it. He willingly takes the accusatory mantle of sinner upon himself, submitting at Calvary to humanity's worst scapegoating and delusionality on the way to Easter Sunday. So, whereas in the fourth and fifth centuries the Monophysites would not acknowledge Jesus's fully human nature (favoring instead a single, divine–human hybrid nature) while the Nestorians kept his humanity firmly separate from his divinity, the Council of Chalcedon (451) endorsed the apparent paradox that Christ was "recognized in two natures, without confusion, without change, without division, without separation; the distinction of natures being in no way annulled by the union, but rather the characteristics of each nature being preserved and coming together to form one person."[31] The practical implication here is that God's Trinitarian "insides" are forever open to the flawed reality of human beings.

As for purity, then, we need to understand that God's holiness means anything but an insistence on purity as usually conceived.[32] Godly holiness is not about keeping ourselves pure and refusing contact with sin-damaged humanity, either in the Church or among those who refuse to have anything to do with the Church. And it is not to insist on a purer, invisible Church. Rather, holiness entails loving solidarity with the unlovely, the sinful, and the compromised, whereby God forms the Church into the image of Jesus Christ, the friend of sinners (Matthew 11:19, Luke 7:34).

As a result, there must be no fast-track out of historical complexity and human fallibility for the people of God. Instead, and in the meantime, the actual Church is what we have, as a sign that God is no enemy of human beings but instead bears with them in love and works with them, among them, at one with them in Jesus Christ. This level of identification might help us to imagine how Jesus can be so radically identified with his Church that the vine and the branches constitute one organism.

The Church is thus an immersive sign for the world, bearing this radical, nonpurist, and hence singularly liberating alternative holiness. It is not an invisible or blueprint Church of discarnate ideals but one of real flesh-and-blood people. The treasure of Jesus Christ thus committed to the Church is the paradigm of how God chooses to work with human beings and their history more generally, beyond what our sins and follies would indicate. The only "proof" of all this is the unassailable fact that faith abides and bears fruit in changed lives. The treasure is still being found in earthen vessels.

For Reflection and Discussion

- Have recent abuse scandals changed how you feel about the Church?

- What challenges do women face in the Church?

- What is the Church like for LGBTQIA+ people?

- Is there an "invisible Church" or only the "visible" one? Is that as it should be?

CHAPTER

5

Watermarks
of the Church

And I hold in veneration,
For the love of Him alone,
Holy Church as His creation,
And her teachings as His own.

John Henry Newman
from "Firmly I Believe and Truly"

I prefer an ecclesiology in a minor key, not a grand ecclesiology.
Edward Schillebeeckx
I Am a Happy Theologian, 74.

At the level of human understanding, Christian orthodoxy is never far from paradox. God is one, yet in a threefold way. The world is God's good creation, yet in its created freedom there is room for suffering and evil. God is not part of creation, yet is present throughout that creation. Likewise, God is at work on the inside of human work and creativity. The incarnation represents the clearest instance, with Jesus recognized as at once both divine and human. And this apparent paradoxicality—this *mystery* if you like—also applies to the Church. It is a divine initiative yet a human institution; it is God's gift yet also a human task; it is and forever will be Christ's beloved bride, though clearly not always a faithful one. This last apparent paradox, with its contrast between heavenly treasure and earthen vessels, is likely to be the Christian claim that most perplexes and upsets people. Theological ideas are one thing, but a Church that lets people down, sometimes demonstrating little of the truth and grace that it is called to embody, readily becomes a scandal to faith.

Given these considerations, how could we—how should we—talk about the actual Church as one, holy, catholic, and apostolic? According to the Nicene Creed, the Church is defined by these four "marks" as an article of faith—or, better I think, by these four *watermarks*. A mark can be obvious, though a watermark might not be. It might jump out at us, though again, we might fail to see it. *A watermark is a mark with some mystery about it.* And so with the Church: its watermarks may not always be obvious, though faith will discern them.

The Church's Gift, Task, and Promise— Introducing the Watermarks

The four canonical watermarks—one, holy, catholic, and apostolic—began as descriptions but were soon being used polemically. The Catholic Church reserved the marks to itself, and with this in mind, Protestants sought to augment or qualify them—Stephen Pickard points out that they have never worked reliably as units of measurement.[1]

Philip Melanchthon (1497–1560) and Martin Luther (1483–1546) insisted on two new marks or "notes" in Lutheranism's Augsburg Confession (1530): the proper preaching of the gospel and administration of the sacraments.[2] These additions need not displace the traditional four, however. Writing influentially on the marks from across the Catholic-Protestant divide were two Tübingen friends, Hans Küng and Jürgen Moltmann. For Küng, the four traditional marks of Catholicism do not mean anything without Protestantism's proper stress on faithfulness in word and sacrament.[3] While for Moltmann, the four credal marks and the Reformation call for a sounder approach to word and sacrament simply represent different perspectives: "A church in which the gospel is purely preached and the sacraments are rightly used *is* the one, holy, catholic and apostolic church."[4]

But then further variations set in, making it increasingly clear that from the sixteenth century onwards, no single Christian church could entirely compass the Christian impulse.[5] Following on from articles in the Augsburg Confession, Luther proposed seven "notes":

1. The preaching of the true word of God.
2. The proper administration of baptism.
3. The correct form of the Lord's Supper.
4. The power of the keys.[6]
5. The lawful vocation and ordination of ministers.
6. Prayer and the singing of psalms in the vernacular.
7. Persecutions.[7]

At the other radical end of the Reformation—and well outside the Lutheran comfort zone—Menno Simons (1496–1561) in Germany then John Smyth (1554–1612) in England offered a Baptist ecclesiology that could be summarized in six interrelated principles: "(1) An existentially authentic community, (2) made so by Christ's spiritual presence in the activity of the Spirit, (3) ratified in an ongoing covenant, (4) effected in a small congregation, (5) manifested by common discipline, so that (6) the whole church is constituted by these discrete and autonomous communities."[8] This pattern reflected a rejection of infant baptism, the Catholic mass, parishes, dioceses, and the idea of a more encompassing institutional Church, with a suspicion of worldly engagement and the use of external forms in worship (i.e., by both Catholics and mainstream Protestants).

In the last century, Pentecostalism further pushed the bounds of Protestant ecclesiology by introducing its concept of a "Full Gospel," which it regards as having been lost by other types of Christianity. It comprises five elements: in addition to justification by faith followed subsequently by sanctification, as elsewhere in classical Protestantism, Pentecostals add the availability of bodily healing for all, Christ's eventual return to the earth, and a second baptism—that of the Holy Spirit— evidenced by the gift of speaking in tongues (ecstatic speech).[9]

All these Protestant developments emphasize concrete outcomes beyond definitions and promises. But so too with the four classical marks in more recent ecumenical discussion. For Moltmann, they are "messianic predicates of the church in the perspective of the coming Kingdom," yes, but if they are statements of faith and promise, "they also lead to *statements of action*."[10] His particular conviction is that oneness, holiness, catholicity, and apostolicity must find new bearings today as churches take up the cause of freedom and justice, with partisanship on behalf of the oppressed.[11] Leonardo Boff would concur from the perspective of Latin American Liberation theology, resisting a monolithic and conservative Catholic conception of the Church and its marks in favor of welcoming local diversity, empowering the poor and downtrodden to take a place of leadership in the Church's life and mission, emphasizing concrete witness for justice, and considering the lay-led base Christian communities to be fundamental.[12] Hans Küng concludes that the marks only serve as a sign if they are being visibly played out: "Unity, holiness, catholicity and apostolicity are not only gifts, granted to the Church by God's grace, but at the same time tasks which it is vital for the Church to fulfill in a responsible way."[13]

Stephen Pickard proposes that these four marks should be considered as emergent properties—as both "originative gift" and "unfolding destiny"—with the aim of keeping some dynamism and creative plasticity in the discussion, so that the marks do not become ossified categories.[14] "Emergent property" is a scientific term referring to a sudden change of state, latent in a physical system but only realized when changing conditions pass a particular threshold.

This is a stimulating suggestion, though I am concerned that emergent properties have either emerged or they have not. Phase changes are an example, from solid to liquid to gas. Another is the phenomenon of superconductivity in a metal. This only happens when its electrons form Cooper pairs—at a particular temperature approaching absolute zero—which will then flow perpetually through a supercooled circuit after an external current has been withdrawn.[15] The water is either frozen or not, while the electrons will either flow unhindered or they will not. In both cases, it depends on the temperature.

However, while the Church's marks may be more or less clearly expressed, they can never be merely latent; their presence or otherwise does not depend on conditions. Hence, my preferred image is the watermark, which is permanently there even if it is not always obvious. So, unlike emergent properties, which are latent though not necessarily manifest, its watermarks are forever on the Church's face—as a promise, as an encouragement, as a calling, and as a reminder of the Church's perennial ability to surprise us, even when its failures have been made all too clear. These watermarks are forever imprinted on the actual Church, for all its faults.

Here I return to my wider point about the actual Church being the only proper subject of ecclesiology. As Harald Hegstad concludes,

> The fact that the actual and present church is the real church means this is the *only* church. Whatever God does not achieve in and through this church, is not to be realized in an invisible and hidden church. If the church's call to unity, holiness and catholicity is to be fulfilled, it is to be fulfilled in this church. If the calling

of God upon the church is to be realized, it must be completed by this church. What makes this possible is the reality that the church is not left by itself.[16]

I will now consider these four watermarks in turn, which constitute the actual Church's gift, task, and promise.

Oneness, Unity, and the Nontribal Tribe

John's Jesus declares in his so-called high priestly prayer that the oneness of Christians is both a mark of the Church's mystical abiding in his own divine life *and* its missional starting point, praying "that they may all be one. As you, Father, are in me and I am in you, may they also be in us, so that the world may believe that you have sent me" (John 17:21). In my own terms, from Chapter 3, such Church unity is a matter both of systole and diastole. Likewise, what Hans Küng describes as "The most pertinent summary of what the unity of the Church is according to the New Testament"[17] appears in the Pauline writer's following entreaty:

> I therefore, the prisoner in the Lord, beg you to lead a life worthy of the calling to which you have been called, with all humility and gentleness, with patience, bearing with one another in love, making every effort to maintain the unity of the Spirit in the bond of peace. There is one body and one Spirit, just as you were called to the one hope of your calling, one Lord, one faith, one baptism, one God and Father of all, who is above all and through all and in all (Ephesians 4:1–6).

We are dealing here with something essential rather than optional. Nevertheless, Church unity has become optional for many, especially in Free Church (e.g., Baptist) and Pentecostal contexts where each congregation is a church (i.e., rather than part of a larger, more-encompassing regional, national, or global body). These Christians rightly value harmony within the congregation as a key expression of the unity principle, though they are wary of wider unity, especially with churches that diverge significantly from their own norms. As the Finnish Evangelical theologian Veli-Matti Kärkkäinen explains, "the Free churches think that the personal faith of individuals is the key to unity, whereas all other churches—while not denying the role of personal faith—ground unity in the church and tradition."[18]

The case of the Catholic Church is especially significant. In 1928, Pope Pius XI declared in his encyclical *Mortalium Animos* (meaning "the minds of mortals") that there can be no unity between churches that is not visible, which necessarily includes unity in faith and Church government. Hence, the only genuine unity is via a return to the bosom of mother Church.[19] As Pope Pius memorably put it,

> Let, therefore, the separated children draw nigh to the Apostolic See, set up in the City which Peter and Paul, the Princes of the Apostles, consecrated by their blood; to that See, We repeat, which is "the root and womb whence the Church of God springs," not with the intention and the hope that "the Church of the living God, the pillar and ground of the truth" will cast aside the integrity of the faith and tolerate their errors, but, on the contrary, that they themselves submit to its teaching and government. Would that it were Our happy lot to do that which so many of Our predecessors could not, to embrace with fatherly affection those children, whose unhappy separation from Us We now bewail.[20]

Thankfully, the Second Vatican Council (Vatican II, 1962–1965) set aside this language of "separated children," who were formerly regarded as wrongheaded individuals—as heretics and schis-matics—in favor of acknowledging the reality of grace-imbued ecclesial communities (separated at the Reformation) along with sister churches (Eastern Orthodox)—with the consoling addi-tion that, somewhere between these poles, and "Among those in which Catholic traditions and institutions in part continue to exist, the Anglican Communion occupies a special place."[21] At Vatican II, Rome also abandoned the claim that it alone *is* the true Church of Jesus Christ, favoring a qualified but still exclu-sive variant: that the true Church *subsists in* (i.e., exists integrally within) the Catholic Church.

In what Avery Dulles described as one of the most signif-icant achievements of Vatican II,[22] and representing a nota-ble departure in tone from *Mortalium Animos*, the "Dogmatic Constitution on the Church, *Lumen Gentium*" (meaning "The Light of the Nations"), refers to

the one Church of Christ, which in the Creed is pro-fessed as one, holy, catholic, and apostolic, which our Saviour, after His Resurrection, commissioned Peter to shepherd, and him and the other apostles to extend and direct with authority, which He erected for all ages as "the pillar and mainstay of the truth." This Church con-stituted and organized in the world as a society, subsists in the Catholic Church, which is governed by the suc-cessor of Peter and by the Bishops in communion with him, although many elements of sanctification and of truth are found outside of its visible structure. These elements, as gifts belonging to the Church of Christ, are forces impelling toward catholic unity.[23]

Rather than being the true Church, then, the claim is now that the true Church *exists within* the Church of Rome. Further, as Andrew Meszaros points out, this means that Church unity is *already present* within the Catholic Church and can still be affirmed despite any empirical disunity.[24] However, what has been called *return ecumenism* remains the only path to participating fully in the Church's oneness—what Anglo-Catholics call "crossing the Tiber."

Coming from that Catholic end of Anglicanism, I long accepted a variant beloved of my kind: the so-called branch theory of Church unity. It holds that the one, holy, catholic, and apostolic Church exists in the world, but with three branches in the three great episcopal traditions: Roman Catholic, Eastern Orthodox, and Anglican. The Anglican Communion effectively formalized this sensibility with what is known as the Chicago-Lambeth Quadrilateral. It was first proposed by the American priest William Reed Huntington and adopted in 1886 by bishops of the Episcopal Church meeting in Chicago. It was then promulgated by the third Lambeth Conference of Anglican bishops in 1888 as the ecumenical standard for Anglicanism in local but also more global overtures toward Christian unity. Resolution 11 declares:

> That, in the opinion of this Conference, the following Articles supply a basis on which approach may be by God's blessing made toward Home Reunion:
>
> a. The Holy Scriptures of the Old and New Testaments, as "containing all things necessary to salvation," and as being the rule and ultimate standard of faith.
>
> b. The Apostles' Creed, as the Baptismal Symbol; and the Nicene Creed, as the sufficient statement of the Christian faith.
>
> c. The two Sacraments ordained by Christ Himself—Baptism and the Supper of the Lord—ministered with unfailing use of Christ's words of Institution, and of the elements ordained by Him.

d. The Historic Episcopate, locally adapted in the methods of its administration to the varying needs of the nations and peoples called of God into the Unity of His Church.[25]

Here we can see a path to unity with the other "Catholic" churches, according to the branch theory, though not without significant grafting being required on their part if Protestant denominations are to be accepted. However, even regarding apparent Anglican closeness to Rome and the Orthodox, Hans Küng asks a searching question: "can these Churches be branches or off-shoots of the same tree when they dissociate themselves from one another?"[26]

So, how are we to think of the divided Church's watermark of oneness or unity today? It is important to remember that multiplicity does not necessarily imply disunity. The New Testament canonizes a diversity of churches—which both issued and were shaped by the various apostolic writings in epistles and Gospels—that were nevertheless united. Küng describes this New Testament Church as neither centralized nor egalitarian nor totalitarian nor monolithic, featuring "fundamentally different historical forms of the one Church, which may all be legitimate."[27] He emphasizes the "existing common ecclesial reality" of their professed unity in Christ as decisive, in spite of their multiplicity[28]—as Kärkkäinen comments on Küng's perspective, this grounding of unity is in God and not in the Church's members, and so the Church's multiplicity is not necessarily a bad thing. Kärkkäinen concludes that "Unity in Christ does not exist despite and in opposition to diversity but is given with and in diversity."[29]

This perspective represents a major feature of ecumenical thought in the twentieth century, allowing the recognition of significant existing unity while Church differences are seen in more secondary terms. Roger Haight calls this new sensibility a "transdenominational ecclesiology," emerging both at the World Council of Churches Assembly at Delhi in 1961 and at Vatican II in 1965. It recognizes that the wellsprings of Christians' shared faith reach deeper than doctrine and hence doctrinal disputes, which therefore "allows churches to find in others what they share in a common transcendent faith despite serious differences."[30] As the Vatican II "Decree on Ecumenism, *Unitatis Redintegratio*" (meaning "Restoration of Unity") puts it, "All the faithful should remember that the more effort they make to live holier lives according to the gospel, the better they will further Christian unity and put it into practice. For the closer their union with the Father, the Word, and the Spirit, the more deeply they will grow in mutual brotherly love."[31]

Küng believes that this drawing together in Christ, which goes beneath the surface of existing divisions, should lead to mutual reception rather than absorption as the model for Church unity.[32] This suggests that unity will be found in the intercommunion of mutually recognized churches, as in the 1992 Porvoo agreement between European Anglican and Lutheran churches, which calls for more than a federation of co-operating churches, though without absorption into one church.[33]

The whole emphasis here is away from institutional narrowness. Penitential openness replaces what was too often a mutually suspicious closed-mindedness. The Orthodox theologian Boris Bobrinskoy captures the requisite mood even though he does not renounce his claim that Eastern Orthodoxy is the true Church: "The desire for unity in the Orthodox Church has to be a kind of suffering, a wound of love and compassion toward a large portion of Christ's Church that is still sacramentally cut off from Orthodox communion in its fulness."[34] This recalls the groaning of all creation for its restoration (Romans 8:22), which Stephen Pickard invokes as providing further impetus to unity in the Church. This restless spirit at work in all things, impelled by the grace of God to remake and fulfill a marred creation, must be manifest in the ecclesial mark of oneness, according to Pickard, issuing not only in Christian union with Christ and in Church unity but also in the Church's integral involvement with wider struggles for a better world and for the integrity of creation.[35]

If the Church is called by God to be the nontribal tribe, as I have claimed, then anxious, self-defining tribalistic rivalry cannot be tolerated between different Christian families. The Church's calling is to experience, model, and foster nontribalistic behavior for a human race that can now destroy itself both by nuclear action and climate inaction. The Church's calling to unity—to making more obvious the unity that it already enjoys in Christ, which includes moving toward greater visible unity—can no longer be optional. If God wants to save the world from itself, Christians need to show the world that God can first save the Church from itself.

The oneness of the Church, then, is a matter of going beyond tribalism to reveal a new way of being tribal, which makes peace and opens a new future for divided humanity. The oneness of all Christians in Christ, abiding in the vine, implies that the naturally and inescapably linguistic, demographic, cultural, historical, and, yes, theological factors that have issued in a multiplicity of Christian expressions cannot degenerate into a sub-Christian tribalism. The spirit that will make this breakthrough possible is that of holiness, the next of our four watermarks.

Alternative Holiness— On Being the Nontribal Tribe

We immediately think of holiness as a personal category, lying somewhere at the interface between spirituality, morality, and boorishness. Indeed, when holiness becomes self-regarding and self-defining, it does become boorish and worse. It falls out of the gospel and the new creation onto more familiar anthropological terrain, where it can cling to categories of pure and impure, of worthy and unworthy, of me-and-mine versus you-and-yours. And what is true for individual Christians is true for Christian corporate personalities in the Church, which can otherwise sink into unreconstructed tribalism.

But here a crucial transformation of perspective takes place, which is so foreign to normal human practice throughout history that we receive it as a gift from God. First in Israel and then in the person of Israel's greatest son, God advanced the human agenda beyond anxious self-definition and spiritual one-upmanship. A human person was born to be the bearer of God's new creation, with dignity and a vocation that did not need to be anxiously hoarded and boasted about. The prophets reminded Israel that being loved and forgiven were now the wellsprings of its identity, enabling thankful loyalty and loving service in place of anxious and peevish self-assertion. Repentance, forgiveness, and clinging to the grace of God brought a new kind of purity that required no one to be perpetually cut off.

As mentioned earlier, the version of holiness and purity exemplified by Jesus represents a radical alternative. Now the sinners become friends of God, with prostitutes and tax collectors to be first through heaven's door (Matthew 21:31), while those who seek to leverage their position in the existing religious framework are leaving themselves behind. The cross is the proof: here is God's holy one stepping willingly into the place of contempt, shame, and curse. Jesus became officially unholy and formally impure, which was necessary if humanity was to find an alternative holiness and purity. In light of the cross, then, the resurrection is not just one more generic miracle. Rather, it is God vindicating a whole new way of being human, beyond the anthropology textbook. The resurrection releases a new Spirit in the world, a new divine reality, which calls forth a new human reality in response—the Church. The Holy Spirit invites the Holy Church to see beyond what humanity typically regards as holiness and purity.

This does not excuse license and moral indifference on the Church's part, but instead it enables a humble self-awareness that is not always blaming others. It is this experience of grace, forgiveness, and new beginnings that allows humans to let go of their anxious self-justification. Instead, it is justification by faith that can displace the anxiously assertive ego. For Moltmann, "The Church is therefore holy precisely at the point where it acknowledges its sins and the sins of mankind and trusts to justification through God."[36]

Christ's alternative holiness works on sinners not to rank them on a scale of holiness but to liberate them from that whole mentality of ranking. "The holiness of the church is not initially the holiness of her members or her cultic assemblies," as Moltmann insists, but instead "it is the holiness of Christ who acts for sinners. Christ sanctifies his Church by justifying it. Consequently the holiness of the church lies in its sanctifying activity."[37] So, instead of putting others down, holiness means building them up, and this on as wide a front as possible—for Stephen Pickard, "Holiness occurs as all things are raised up to their fullness of life in God."[38]

Of course, none of this will necessarily bring comfort or reassurance to those whom the Church has neglected, harmed, or worse. Indeed, some of these will regard all this talk of holiness as a sick joke. But the point I am making is that only as God's creature, God's movement, and God's project in the tangled skein of human motivation could the Church possibly find itself able to be a different sort of human community. Only by learning to receive holiness as a gift from the all-holy God, who is perpetually and patiently drawing us away from all unholiness and ersatz holiness, can the Church gradually become an alternative to every other human group and institution.

The Church's indelible and irrevocable holiness, given in Christ as a gift, is meant to release an answering holiness rather than to excuse unholiness—and we do indeed see genuine holiness playing out among Christians and churches, though not universally and not perfectly. Only this version of holiness is worth the name of Christian—a holiness that means acceptance by God, which then frees the Church from having to establish its own worthiness at the expense of declaring others to be unholy and unworthy. It is precisely when the Church forgets this in favor of anxious egotism and tribalism that it does the damage for which so many rightly reproach it.

For the Church, then, the systole must find its diastole: "Because it *is* holy, it must *be* holy; the indicative brings an imperative."[39] And it is Jesus's alternative version of holiness, which makes the unlovely lovable and the unwelcome welcome, that points through the Church to the world's ultimate destiny in God. As Moltmann explains, "Through continual new conversion and permanent reformation [the Church] testifies to the coming *reformatio mundi* which is already present in the Spirit—the 'new order of all things' in the Kingdom of God."[40]

Moltmann adds that the Church's witness to the Kingdom of God, sharing God's alternative holiness for the sake of a reconfigured world, will be at odds with normal human reckoning. Hence, the Church will suffer, inevitably and inescapably, as a consequence of this scandalously alternative holiness.[41] By extension, the Church's present shame and soul-searching in light of widespread scandals of abuse and coverup might be understood as an experience of God-mandated suffering. It should foster institutional reform and recovery, recalling the Church to its identity and mission for the life of the world.

High-Bandwidth Catholicity

Catholicity has long been a matter of claim and counter-claim, and nowhere more so than between the monolithic Roman Catholic multinational Church and endlessly diversifying Protestant congregationalism. However, a unity that embraces some level of multiplicity has always typified catholicity.[42] Indeed, even the fifth-century "Vincentian Canon," with its classic threefold definition of catholicity as "what has been believed everywhere, always, and by all" can be qualified—as Wolfhart Pannenberg argues, "Nowhere has only that been taught as catholic truth which was believed everywhere, always and by all *in the same form.*"[43] This canon was also subtly recontextualized in a more inclusive way at Vatican II, with the admission that "some and even very many of the significant elements and endowments which together go to build up and give life to the Church itself, can exist outside the visible boundaries of the Catholic Church."[44]

The tendency here is to ecclesially broaden while theologically deepening the definition of catholicity, toward a higher bandwidth conception that preserves apostolic tradition while remaining open to the signs of the times and confident about the contribution of catholic faith to humanity's future.[45] So, being catholic can be seen as a gift, challenge, and responsibility rather than a boast.[46]

The bounds of catholicity are set by God's originating intent in creation, according to Stephen Pickard, for whom "It is the catholic Spirit which broods and hovers over the abyss in Genesis that brings all things into being through the Word which creates human society and forms communities of faith and love."[47] In addition, before catholicity is applied to the Church it emerges from the person and work of Jesus Christ.[48] Hence, for Moltmann, "The Church is related in a missionary way to the whole of mankind because its resurrection hope and its eucharistic prayer include everyone. 'Catholic' is therefore an eminently eschatological definition of the church."[49] This missional aspect of the church's catholicity is crucial. It represents the promise of wholeness coming back into a broken world, chiefly through seeking and restoring the lost, rejected, and oppressed, as Moltmann emphasizes.[50] Where is the bringing together of all things as they should be in Christ without the ones whose rejection Christ voluntarily shares? The catholicity of the whole people of God is the ecclesial expression of this larger catholic project, which awaits its eschatological fulfillment.[51] "Catholic" does, after all, derive from the Greek *kata holos*: "according to the whole."

In the meantime, catholicity does not require monolithic unity and a uniquely extensive reach—as Henri de Lubac memorably reminds us, the Church "was already Catholic in the morning of Pentecost, when all her members could be contained in a small room."[52] The nascent Catholic Church demonstrated its catholicity at Pentecost by holding together the centrality of Christ with the universality of his mission, which was evident in the plurality of its members, revealing the limitless breadth and openness of Christ's rule.[53]

I see catholicity as having a firm center but soft edges— like al dente pasta. With the aforementioned Chicago-Lambeth quadrilateral, I endorse the originary Christian elements of word, baptism and Eucharist, credal affirmation, and the historic episcopate as it has been variously received in different contexts. And, regarding episcopal ministry, this gives me some useful flexibility. For example, it allows me to honor the Petrine primacy—the papacy—as one such contextual expression of episcopal ministry and, to my mind, a highly valuable and desirable one as the Church seeks greater fidelity and unity. But I can also affirm a catholic intent in those Protestant episcopal traditions that did not seek to preserve the so-called historic episcopate or the historical apostolic succession while others did (i.e., of hands being laid on new bishops by previous bishops in unbroken sequence, back to the mists of ecclesial time). The fact that these two approaches within Protestantism are now being reconciled, with historical apostolic succession actually being recovered and restored in some contexts, is an admirably catholic development (more on this in the next section).

Here we see emerging what Hans Küng would call an "evangelical Catholicism."[54] "Being Catholic," he says, "means being ecumenical in the fullest sense."[55] This does not entail the sacrifice of central Catholic principle, though in his willingness to accept some softness at the edges, Küng has always seemed close to Anglican sensibility—after all, he did dedicate the English edition of *The Church* to the then Archbishop of Canterbury, Michael Ramsey.

Regarding this softness at the edges, I endorse Anglican comprehensiveness in being able to tolerate a measure of ambiguity and untidiness. The sixteenth-century Church of England charted its course away from papal authority in an environment where potentially inflammatory doctrinal unresolvedness could not be avoided. Following in that tradition, those of us who have resisted the cultural siren song of invincible certainty can accept (if not always with enthusiasm) some secondary matters being left up in the air. We do not see this as necessarily foreign to the gospel or to the catholic project.

I can even accept Rome's claim that the fullness of catholicity is to be found in the Catholic Church, though to say that it subsists there—that the true Church of Christ exists integrally in the Roman Church like a Platonic form—can risk separating the *true Church* from the plurality and ambiguity of the *actual Church*, which we might call its "graced limitedness." This is something I have been trying to avoid in this book. The Church of Christ must enter the darkness of Easter

Saturday while holding to the degree of catholic clarity that God has always made available to it.

This nontribal spirit is found in so-called Generous Orthodoxy: a new openness to theological mediation across confessional differences but also across the liberal/conservative, left/right divide.[56] It resists polarization and favors the reconciliation of diversity over uniformity, seeking to "work for pluralistic unity within the framework of distinctively Christian belief and practice."[57]

> Many of the theologians associated with this sentiment of theology did not attempt to overcome doctrinal positions by eliminating particularity or their specific confessional tradition. They rather undertook the challenging task of making them fit together in a dynamic tension with the various particularities. Something emerged that was neither "my way or the highway," nor "anything goes."[58]

This is the sort of broadband catholicity that honors the Church's ancient deposit of catholic faith while working ecumenically to rebalance unity and multiplicity—a sign from the Church that is sorely needed in today's global conditions of unmatched danger and possibility. Here is the apostolic task of a truly catholic Church.

Apostolicity—Continuity and Change

The first generation of Christian disciples and the New Testament writings soon following were essential for founding the Church.[59] The Church was "built upon the foundation of the apostles and prophets, with Christ Jesus himself as the cornerstone" (Ephesians 2:20). This is an incontrovertible and even a sobering realization. "He who does not hear the apostles," as Hans Küng uncompromisingly put it, "does not hear the Lord.

There is no route to the Lord that bypasses the apostles."[60] Paul tended to see the apostles as early witnesses to Christ's resurrection, though Luke tightened up the definition by limiting it to Jesus's reconstituted disciple band (Acts 1:21–22) and possibly to Paul (Acts 9:15).[61] Indeed, Paul himself testifies of Christ that "Last of all, as to one untimely born, he appeared also to me" (1 Corinthians 15:8; see also, e.g., Romans 1:1; 2 Corinthians 1:1).

The American Catholic theologian Richard Gaillardetz pointed out that "normative expressions of faith (doctrine) and the authoritative preservation of that faith (apostolic office) did not precede but rather followed upon the ancient conviction that the apostolic faith resided first and foremost in the life of the community."[62] In this spirit, the great World Council of Churches document of 1982, *Baptism, Eucharist and Ministry*, declares that "the primary manifestation of apostolic succession is to be found in the apostolic tradition of the Church as a whole," which is the permanence and continuity of Christ's own mission in which the whole Church participates.[63] BEM (also known as the Lima Document) further declares that:

> The Spirit keeps the Church in the apostolic tradition until the fulfillment of history in the Kingdom of God. Apostolic tradition in the Church means continuity in the permanent characteristics of the Church of the apostles: witness to the apostolic faith, proclamation and fresh interpretation of the Gospel, celebration of baptism and the eucharist, the transmission of ministerial responsibilities, communion in prayer, love, joy and suffering, service to the sick and needy, unity among the local churches and sharing the gifts which the Lord has given to each.[64]

Significantly, the option of emphasizing the apostolic message and mission without paying the same attention to its

ministerial medium has never proved sufficient for the episcopal churches. If apostolicity involves more than legitimation
by historical apostolic succession, resting instead on promise, divine commissioning, and "the evangelical succession,
the continuing and unadulterated proclamation of the gospel
of the risen Christ,"[65] then Rome and like-minded episcopal
churches have still insisted on succession in the historic episcopate to ground and secure that apostolic mission. There is
a danger that the apostolicity of the people of God and their
mission can be lost sight of without appropriate structural support and symbolic reinforcement. For example, in the Catholic tradition of Anglicanism, the apostolic succession of the
episcopate was reasserted by the nineteenth-century Oxford
Fathers precisely because the apostolicity of the Church of
England and its mission was perceived to be under threat.
In Andrew Shanks's assessment, "Apostolicity, as the Oxford
Movement understood it, was essentially a campaigning critique of secular ruling class complacency within the church."[66]

The spirit of generous orthodoxy is evident in how this
visibility of episcopal succession is treated in *Baptism, Eucharist and Ministry*, and in a different context by the Porvoo
Common Statement that puts BEM's recommendations
about apostolic succession and episcopacy into practice. The
challenge is how one might bring two kinds of churches
together. In BEM, the gap between nonepiscopal and episcopal churches is bridged by today's growing mutual recognition of apostolicity—one type of Church has the apostolic
tradition, proclamation, and mission, though with moderators
and superintendents rather than bishops, while the other has
the apostolic tradition, proclamation, and mission with added
symbolic reinforcement from the historic episcopate. Each
is encouraged to acknowledge the apostolicity of the other
despite their differences over bishops,[67] while the nonepiscopal churches are further invited to "realize that the continuity

with the church of the apostles finds profound expression in the successive laying on of hands by bishops and that, though they may not lack the continuity of the apostolic tradition, this sign will strengthen and deepen that continuity." Indeed, BEM goes so far as to suggest that "They may need to recover the sign of the episcopal succession."[68]

This is indeed what happened in the mid-twentieth century when new churches were formed by Anglicans and nonepiscopal Protestants joining together: The Church of South India (1947), then the Church of North India, and the Church of Pakistan (both in 1970). These conducted their ordinations of deacons, priests, and bishops with the intention that after an interim generation or so, their new churches would become "entirely episcopal" in the historic succession, gifted to them by the Anglicans.

The Porvoo context, on the other hand, involves two different versions of episcopacy. European Anglicans all claim the historic episcopal succession, as do the Swedish Lutherans, while other Lutherans such as the Germans and Danes appoint bishops without historic episcopal succession with its unbroken laying on of hands. Porvoo counsels patient mutual recognition in these circumstances, while envisaging the eventual full return of the historic episcopal succession as mutual episcopal ordinations "leaven the whole lump." Porvoo emphasizes other signs of intentional connectedness with the pre-Reformation past that demonstrate the intention to maintain catholic continuity, even without the bishops being in historical succession—namely uninterrupted traditions of parochial and liturgical life, with the shared history of Anglo-Saxon missions to Northern Europe, but especially by the unbroken occupation in Europe of the ancient pre-Reformation dioceses from which the ministry of their bishops cannot be divorced.[69] Thus we have the following remarkably gracious and encouraging statement from Porvoo, which, in my terms, is thoroughly nontribal:

> The mutual acknowledgement of our churches and ministries is theologically prior to the use of the sign of the laying on of hands in the historic succession. Resumption of the use of the sign does not imply an adverse judgement on the ministries of those churches which did not previously make use of the sign. It is rather a means of making more visible the unity and continuity of the church at all times and in all places.[70]

In recent decades, the same generous orthodoxy has softened the sad history of relations between the Churches of Rome and Canterbury through the Anglican-Roman Catholic International Commission (ARCIC) and its several agreed statements, in parallel with the International Anglican-Roman Catholic Commission for Unity and Mission (IARCCUM).[71] However, we are still a long way from Rome recognizing Anglican churches alongside the Eastern Orthodox as valid catholic sister churches in the historic apostolic succession.

The point of this chapter, following the last with its discussion of treasure in earthen vessels, has been to interpret today's actual "Church of churches"—the one that we all see and know—according to the Church's four classic marks enshrined in the Nicene Creed: one, holy, catholic, and apostolic. My claim is that this fallible human entity, which every honest and attentive Christian knows the Church to be, is at the same time formed and sustained by God's love and promise. This represents yet one more apparent Christian paradox, and in that sense, it is fitting to talk about the mystery of the Church. Rather than "marks of the Church," then, I have proposed the image of watermarks—they are real, and forever present, yet they may not always be obvious.

This approach does not provide the Church with excuses though it does offer it reassurances. There will always be more to the Church than its worst features might indicate. The Kingdom of God will never lack the Church's concrete witness in the travail of history. And part of that witness—a witness the world needs—is that today's universal spirit of tribalism, which threatens to bring our world undone, is presented with a nontribal alternative and, with that, a potentially more hopeful future. If we forget this promise, we might only register the Church's faults and not see those many countervailing graces that the honest and attentive must also acknowledge. Many wish that things could be better in the Church, but we also know that things could be a lot worse. "Saints their watch are keeping" indeed.

For Reflection and Discussion

- Are Church divisions something we should be concerned about? Why?

- What would an attractive Christian holiness look like?

- In what way is your church catholic, and you yourself?

- Is the apostolic succession of bishops worth having? Why?

Come and See

Nathanael said to him, "Can anything good come out of Nazareth?"
Philip said to him, "Come and see."

John 1:46

Come to him, a living stone, though rejected by mortals yet chosen
and precious in God's sight, and like living stones, let yourselves be
built into a spiritual house, to be a holy priesthood, to offer spiritual
sacrifices acceptable to God through Jesus Christ.

1 Peter 2:4–5

[Jesus] said to them, "I have earnestly desired to eat this Passover
with you before I suffer. . . ."

Luke 22:15

I t is unlikely that talking up any personal advantages that
the Church might offer will attract many modern people
to it, let alone convince them to stay. If Western churches
play to today's subjective spiritual impulse, they risk being out-
done by something more personally amenable that delivers
satisfaction more reliably. And when worship is dull, uncon-
vinced, uninspiring, and all the other disappointing things that
typify many mainstream congregations, it will not do to tell
people that it is still somehow good for them to be there. This
is like telling children that eating broccoli is good for them—it
is unlikely to provide the requisite motivation. What works is
the change of perspective that faith brings, which needs to be
evoked so that people are awakened to the presence of something compelling. If you must be a committed vegetarian or
vegan to welcome the sight of plain steamed broccoli, which

I firmly believe to be the case, likewise, the dawning of faith through encountering Jesus Christ and his gospel is what will open minds and hearts to the Church.

The Treasure and the Pearl

Jesus's parables of the treasure and the pearl of great price (Matthew 13:44–46) prove instructive. Hidden stashes of wealth were apparently not unknown in those pre-usury days before bank interest, and if you were able to acquire the land, then any treasure you had previously found secreted there was yours. With that end in view, the necessary outlay would hardly register. Likewise, in the second of these parables, the collector finds their long-dreamt-of prize, the pearl of great price, and of course any serious collector or alert speculator knows that money is no object at a moment like that. But often preachers work against the grain of these parables, exhorting their hearers to greater sacrifice to acquire the prize as if that were the key point. Whereas the logic of these big finds is that once we realize just what it is that lies before us, we will need no encouragement to do whatever is necessary to make it ours. So, the preacher's proper task is to evoke the attractiveness of God's Kingdom so that hearers get excited and want to be part of it. Joining the Church is like buying the field or the pearl of great price once the prize has begun to seize the imagination. And being part of God's reign in Jesus Christ is that prize.

I return now to the young Dietrich Bonhoeffer's persevering exhortation, as discussed in Chapter 2, that Church attendance should be an unquestioned norm for Christians. I agree, but how might people be brought to see things that way? While this approach would have made more sense a century ago, when Christian and societal norms were still woven fine, today's lack of a Western cultural location for churchgoing now makes that practice stand out. It is like choosing to commute on foot, by bicycle, or on public transport when it would be quicker and more convenient to drive. Unless, that is, motorists find themselves drawn seriously to environmentalism and determine to reduce their greenhouse gas emissions, whereupon they could well start leaving the car at home, or choose not to have one at all. So too with the Church: if vegetarianism or veganism might awaken you to the delights of broccoli, or a conversion to environmental values might put you on a bicycle or on public transport, so too might some dawning of Christian faith be necessary before the Church's claims can be felt.

For Bonhoeffer, to regard churchgoing as a means of satisfying people's psychological needs, for providing them with other advantages, or for helping them to meet a moral obligation represents a fundamental misunderstanding: "to do so would mean relinquishing from the very outset the right to have one's basic premises."[1] That is, it would mean subordinating the theological to the sociological and the substantive to the functional. But then, Bonhoeffer does introduce confirming experiences, though at a different level, and in a distinct context. He refers to "a genuine experience of the church," which comes through faith. As Bonhoeffer explains,

> Our age is not short on experiences but on *faith*. But only faith creates a genuine experience of the church. Thus we think it more important for our age to be led into the faith in God's church-community than to have experiences squeezed out of it that as such are of no use, but that will come about of their own accord whenever faith in the sanctorum communio has been found.[2]

This represents a repositioning of experience, which, apart from faith, is not necessarily a reliable guide when it comes to Church and churchgoing. Psychologically satisfying experiences for those who might find themselves in church, or that may have been promised as a way of getting them there, are of limited worth in fostering long-term commitment. But the experience of faith is a different matter.

It is absolutely not about the cultivation of emotional intensity, which is today's standard proposal for improving on ordinary, very likely underwhelming Christian worship. Yet such hyped intensity risks playing into distorted versions of the sacred, which can be exclusivist, dismissive of the ill-fitting, and hence violent-tending—as James Alison points out, a quiet Eucharist represents the complete ritual antithesis to a Nuremberg rally. It may not be exciting or productive of great fellow-feeling, but it does help to cultivate the sort of calmed nonviolent imagination that being a nontribal tribe requires.[3]

This is surely a chicken-and-egg situation. Faith leads some people to church and keeps them there, while for others, it is engagement with the Church and its praxis, in one form or another, that awakens faith. Sometimes both grow up together, with newcomers drawn to the Church by a nascent faith that is then nurtured and grown in the Church until they are ready for sacramental initiation and come to belong. Liturgically linked catechumenal processes of guided exploration, intentional Christian formation, and baptismal initiation work on this time-honored expectation, reviving while updating a widespread approach to initiation from the early Church. In any event, the crucial thing—the experience that Bonhoeffer does endorse—is an encounter with Jesus Christ and his gospel that makes subsequent Church involvement seem not only possible but imperative.

The question then becomes one of how this happens—how is this faith evoked, what role does the Church play, and what part of the Church? Pope Francis offers leadership on this issue with his 2022 Apostolic Letter, "*Desiderio Desideravi*, On the Liturgical Formation of the People of God." The title is Latin for the first four words of Jesus's declaration at the last supper: "I have earnestly desired to eat this Passover with you before I suffer . . ." (Luke 22:15). Apart from all the other reasons given for why people should go to church, and regardless of whatever claims might be made for the advantages or efficacy of churchgoing, the Pope declares that Jesus's invitation to us is primary. Jesus earnestly wants us to join him at the Lord's table—to meet him and to know him in the Eucharistic fellowship of his beloved people.

This is the same Lord who feeds the multitude in the wilderness (Matthew 14:13–21), who invites the poor, crippled, blind, and lame to his table (Luke 14:21), who surprises and delights the wedding guests at Cana with his lavish provision of wine for the party (John 2:1–11), who invites his dispirited disciples to share a meal on the shore after the resurrection (John 21:1–17), and who reveals himself in the breaking of the bread after breaking open God's word on the Emmaus road (Luke 24:13–35). All these are formational narratives widely understood to have been crafted with the Eucharist in mind. Jesus, as host, invites all sorts of people to his table, where they will be taught, fed, and drawn into his narrative. The converting power of this encounter is evident in the Emmaus story, where the experience and understanding of the disciples are re-constituted, with the Eucharistic meal representing the apex of revelation. In all these cases, Jesus meets people and brings them together in the faith and equally in the Church, just as in the *Desiderio Desideravi* text of Luke 22:15.

As the liturgical scholar Rita Ferrone points out concerning this Apostolic Letter, "Francis's exposition begins with desire—not our desire, but the desire of Jesus. The letter starts by recalling Jesus's earnest desire to eat the Passover meal with his disciples and, by extension, with all people through time. The point here is that the whole program of liturgy originates in God's action, not our own. If we miss this foundational fact, we will miss everything else."[4]

I referred to the treasure and pearl parables as intended to awaken this desire for God's Kingdom. Here in *Desiderio Desideravi,* there is a related approach that does not begin with awakening our desire but first declares Jesus's desire for us—to invite us, feed us, and know us. Of course, as René Girard has taught us, our desire is always awakened by another's desire, so Jesus's desire to eat the Passover with us will awaken our desire in return. This can make us want to sit down at table with him and our fellow invitees, and to become part of his fellowship in the Eucharistic Church.

Pope Francis explains that "The Liturgy guarantees for us the possibility of such an encounter." No doubt wishing to point beyond depleted notions of the Eucharist as a mere memorial, and with the theme of the Eucharist as the continuation of Jesus's many transformative personal encounters in mind, he goes on to insist that

> For us a vague memory of the Last Supper would do no good. We need to be present at that Supper, to be able to hear [Jesus's] voice, to eat his Body and to drink his Blood. We need Him. In the Eucharist and in all the sacraments we are guaranteed the possibility of encountering the Lord Jesus and of having the power of his Paschal Mystery reach us. The salvific power of the sacrifice of Jesus, his every word, his every gesture, glance, and feeling reaches us through the celebration of the sacraments. I am Nicodemus, the Samaritan woman at the well, the man possessed by demons at Capernaum, the paralytic in the house of Peter, the sinful woman pardoned, the woman afflicted by haemorrhages, the daughter of Jairus, the blind man of Jericho, Zacchaeus, Lazarus, the thief and Peter both pardoned. The Lord Jesus who dies no more, who lives forever with the signs of his Passion continues

to pardon us, to heal us, to save us with the power of the sacraments. It is the concrete way, by means of his incarnation, that he loves us. It is the way in which he satisfies his own thirst for us that he had declared from the cross. (Jn 19:28)[5]

Discerning Jesus's Invitation

Pope Francis does acknowledge, however, that the modern Western imagination is not ideally suited to discerning this invitation in the Church's Eucharist. The beauty and wonder of this invitation is neither aesthetic nor necessarily obvious. In particular, Francis laments today's spiritual worldliness and subjectivism that "poison" this discernment.[6] So, he emphasizes "the need for a serious and vital liturgical formation,"[7] in a call indebted to the twentieth-century liturgical movement that emphasized the teaching and converting power of the liturgy for God's gathered people. That is, once its significance has been grasped—once the spiritual astonishment of what is concretely taking place before and among us both amazes and captures us.

One might discern a model of that formation in how Luke's Emmaus narrative concludes. The first element is a reordering of experience and expectation that takes place for the disciples along the journey of faith with Jesus as he breaks open the word. The decisive revelation follows at table, when Jesus breaks the Eucharistic bread. But then the disciples return to Jerusalem, and the Church begins sharing stories of encountering the risen Jesus that fill out the revelation (Luke 24:33–35). Word, sacrament, and communal sharing represent the linked liturgical and ecclesial elements that are prefigured in the Emmaus text, whereby the risen Jesus among his people points forward to their collective life and mission (Luke 24:36–53). The resultant communal solidarity and sharing of faith stories necessarily form part of this picture and of church life thereafter.

This recalls the emphasis of Czech Catholic priest, theologian, and Soviet-era dissident Tomáš Halík on today's Church needing to take spiritual seekers and their experiences seriously, "not to push the seekers back into already existing structures of the church but through mutual dialogue to enrich and to enlarge the existing structures so as to integrate the experiences in the treasure of faith."[8] Indeed, this insight is behind the renewing impetus toward Synodality in the Catholic Church today, challenging patronizing clericalism in favor of lay spiritual growth, with a greater sense of lay participation in the Eucharist and a more dialogical approach to church life, discipline, and governance.

A helpful Gospel text for resolving in our minds the relationship between Jesus's invitation and the Church's role in mediating that invitation is the story of Lazarus, whom Jesus raises from the dead (John 11:38–44). He calls the dead man out, but Lazarus remains wrapped head to toe in his graveclothes. He is not yet free to inhabit the new life that Jesus desires to share with him. So, the Church is called on to help: "Jesus said to them, 'Unbind him, and let him go'" (John 11:44). The Church—the nontribal tribe—is meant to help people find the more comprehensive, richer vision of life that Jesus earnestly desires to share with them. People have always sought and properly expected this from the Church: "They came to Philip . . . and said to him, 'Sir, we wish to see Jesus'" (John 12:21). But if the Church cannot show Jesus to seekers, if his earnest desire to eat the Passover with us is muted or blocked by the Church, if Bonhoeffer's "genuine experience of the church" is not on offer, so that Newbigin's congregational hermeneutic of the gospel is stillborn, then the consequences are obvious. Few, if any, will find a treasure or a pearl of great price laid out before them for the taking.

However, if the Church succeeds at this, we have the answer to Nathanael's skepticism, in John 1:46. When invited to meet Jesus, Nathanael asks dismissively whether anything good could come from Nazareth. We can picture the sneer on Nathanael's face. It is that of many "cultured despisers" when confronted by the claims of Christianity and especially of the Church. Philip can simply reply, "come and see." Come and see where God makes the reign of God visible and tangible. Come and see where mission is based on encountering an inner radiance, as Boris Bobrinskoy claims on behalf of his Eastern Orthodox tradition.[9] Come and see, with Jürgen Moltmann, "the martyrs, who in the visible fellowship of the crucified Jesus testified to his invisible glory."[10]

For Graham Tomlin, the Church's witness is first and foremost that it represents a new kind of community as described in Ephesians 4, the most ecclesial of New Testament passages:

> Here, the bottom line is truthfulness, transparency and honesty (Ephesians 4.25). Yes, it is sometimes painful to be truthful, but members of this new community pledge to be honest and straightforward with one another. Here, anger is dealt with quickly, and it is not allowed to fester, lest it turn into stone-cold bitterness (4.26–27). Burglars don't just stop stealing; they start giving. They find themselves transformed into part of the solution rather than the problem of a broken world—they change from parasites on society to agents of social improvement as they learn to give generously to those in need (4.28). There is a determination here not to undermine or demean others, but instead to use words positively, to encourage, affirm and bless (4.29). People learn the skill of forgiveness by learning first how much they have been forgiven by God, and how much that pardon cost (4.32).[11]

Here we recall Newbigin's claim, addressed in Chapter 3, that the congregation is the only hermeneutic of the gospel. I argued that the wider Church, with its saints, theologians, and leaders, is no less important. However, a spiritually healthy congregation that inhabits and mediates Jesus's invitation to the Lord's table, and that can form Christians in the requisite new way of seeing and acting, is ideally placed to issue the invitation "come and see."

Post-Church Christianity, or, the New Invisible Church

And now to address the prospect of a post-Church Christianity. I see it arising in a new face-to-face variant in the West, but also in online formats involving either passive viewing of livestreamed worship or else interactive Christian gatherings—even congregations—meeting on Zoom, and now in the metaverse. To begin, I will set out the options, then go on to raise five fundamental concerns that I have about these developments. Basically, I do not regard these options as properly part of the Church, able to adequately mediate Jesus's invitation—his gift, task, and promise.

There is the in-person variant, with a major Anglican move underway to accommodate it. Some English Christians, with official encouragement from Church of England leadership, are opting out of churchgoing in favor of lay-led home fellowships, with bible study, prayer, song, and no priests necessarily involved, even when such groups choose to continue some sort of sacramental life. This is a mission-shaped Church approach, heavily promoted in Evangelical circles and now gaining ground in the wake of COVID lockdowns. The attitude here would be that traditional parish life and worship, with their incarnational emphasis, are tangential and distracting, so that a simpler, more authentic, and more accessible form of Christian gathering is to be preferred. Yet this assessment wilfully dismisses so much social and spiritual capital that priests and lay people are still building up through many parishes in the Church of England, though these are being increasingly talked down, asset stripped, and bypassed.[12]

And then there is the digital church. It appeared with the arrival of new technology for online meetings, livestreaming, and virtual reality that coalesced with COVID lockdowns. On a Sunday in Lent 2023 we attended the main Sunday Eucharist at Washington National (Episcopal) Cathedral in a congregation of perhaps 250, yet my friend in Hawaii who regularly watches that event on the Cathedral's YouTube channel reported 1100 viewers (participants?) online. They refer to this as the "Digital Cathedral," which is now an established part of the National Cathedral's ministry (and of its income stream). Similar examples can be found in England and elsewhere.

One can go further. I think of a Baptist congregation in Melbourne whose long-term pastor has a graduate degree in liturgy from a Catholic university, and whose weekly Eucharist has a strong post-Vatican II Catholic feel while still being recognizably Baptist (the pastor describes himself as Bapto-Catholic). Their worship is wonderfully engaging and deeply appreciated by the small but loyal congregation. Except that since COVID, they have gone entirely online with a well-curated Zoom Eucharist, for which everyone puts out their own bread and wine at home, with preachers Zooming in from around the country and occasionally from further afield. When it is over, the pastor moderates an hour's worth of breakout groups, shuffling online participants every twenty minutes so that everyone gets to talk with everyone else. This congregation—for which I have preached online— has decided not to meet in their building any longer and to only gather in person for occasional social events. They say that a major reason for their decision is that they maintain closer and more meaningful contact with each other through this new medium, but also that it makes staying involved easier for the elderly and those who live at a distance.

But there is yet one more stage beyond meeting exclusively online. I was informed that a staff member at Virginia Theological Seminary hosts a congregation in the metaverse, where everyone has their avatar. I subsequently did an internet search for "churches in the metaverse" and found a slew of material, including a number of actual "churches" to join. Then I followed a hint and searched under "Christian metaverse," finding more material, including a reference to this as the "Netflix of Evangelism." I also found a suggestion that this virtual Christianity may overtake the megachurch phenomenon—if so, it may well constitute a new stage in Church history. Apparently, these gatherings are highly immersive for participants sitting at home wearing their virtual reality headsets.[13] But with this latest metaverse model, we have lost what is on offer even in that Bapto-Catholic online congregation.

The first of my five fundamental concerns about these new post-Church approaches applies specifically to what we might call the digital and virtual turns. The whole logic of catholic Christianity is incarnational, personal, sacramental, earthed, and communal, while the digital and virtual options turn away from such physicality and risk falling back into Gnosticism— the perennial Christian heresy claiming that saving knowledge is enough and that physicality is unimportant, even a hindrance. This concern is considerably heightened when we consider the possibility of a church that sees virtual reality as preferable to the reality in which God became incarnate. Though, if some Christians effectively limit their conception of God's incarnation to words in the Bible, perhaps the switch to virtual reality has already been flipped.

My second concern here is missional. Today's Church in the West needs to provide a counter-witness to consumerism, which has extended its reach to commodify spirituality.[14] The sometimes-demanding requirement of meeting together and making a go of it as a Christian congregation—learning the range of new Christian life skills that Ephesians 4 takes for granted—is relinquished if we approach Christianity more-or-less passively and remotely, with an off switch. In fairness, however, I readily admit that existing congregational life can fail to provide such Christian formation compared to some online versions, like that online Baptist congregation in Melbourne. Though I wonder whether that could only be possible because significant Christian formation in word and sacrament had already taken place among those Baptists when they used to meet in person—that is, because they were already a well-established and mature congregation before they moved online.

My third concern applies both to newer in-person fellowships that withdraw from the wider, gathered Church along with the digital and virtual options. I fear that all these are retreating from publicness. Since the Enlightenment, the location of religion in the modern West is no longer in the public square, but in neutral private spaces where religious people can pursue their favored narratives and practices without disrupting mainstream secular priorities.[15] So, does the abandonment of parish and public liturgy represent a retreat from publicness in the direction of invisibility and disengagement? Indeed, is the digital and even more so this virtual turn a new version of the catacombs, where early Christians once hid themselves from a threatening world? In all these cases—in-person groups of Christians abandoning the Church, along with digital and even VR options—I fear that a new version of the invisible Church is emerging.

And with that comes my fourth concern: all invisible Church thinking involves being suspicious and dismissive of the actual Church. This happened at the Reformation and

subsequently whenever new Christian splinter groups with-
drew from larger bodies. They did so out of concern that their
parent body was no longer either "sound" enough, pure enough,
or up to the task. The home-based Evangelical fellowships
that some are suggesting should now constitute an alternative
version of the Church of England—perhaps with a niche location in the parent body's governance structure while retain-
ing almost total independence for their new "mission-shaped
Church"—are in effect breakaway conventicles. Purely online
fellowships, whether interactive, virtual (and hence aiming at
greater immersion), or just a matter of tuning in, might be seen
as limiting cases of such detachment.

Hence my fifth concern: What do these post-Church phe-
nomena have to do with the one, holy, catholic, and apostolic
Church? How are they related to the Church that has made
its way in more-or-less visible continuity for two millennia
and, in many places today, is visibly, doggedly continuing to
pursue its mission and work toward unity? These new trends
are abandoning all that for something more purely, individually, privately, nontraditionally, and nonecclesially "Christian."
How do you say, "I believe in one, holy, catholic and apostolic
Church" when you refuse to have anything to do with that
Church? For instance, when you opt out of its public celebra-
tions of word and sacrament for a private fellowship of the
like-minded—which may be in a separated group, perhaps via
Zoom or even in VR—or if you simply prefer to watch livestreamed church on YouTube when the mood takes you?

Post-Church Christianity cannot provide the environment for
optimally encountering Jesus's earnest desire to join him at the
Lord's table, and to become the nontribal tribe. That requires
a Church of real flesh-and-blood people sharing that desire as
they make their stand together in the real world—with all the
demanding yet potentially formative challenges that brings. I

readily admit that I am likely to be doing some individuals and groups a disservice with these assessments, though I remain convinced that this post-Church Christianity is doing the actual Church and its mission a disservice.

For Reflection and Discussion

- Why do we call the Eucharist a celebration? Does it look like one?

- Where is Jesus in the Eucharist, what is he doing, and what does he want?

- "Sir, we wish to see Jesus" (John 12:21). How would you reply?

- How unfair is the author being about what he calls post-Church options (i.e., swapping church for a home group, a Zoom or VR congregation, or watching livestreamed services)?

Conclusion

Let all mortal flesh keep silence
And with fear and trembling stand;
ponder nothing earthly-minded,
for with blessing in his hand
Christ our God to earth descending
comes full homage to demand.

from the Liturgy of St James, c. fourth century,
via The English Hymnal, *1906*

I draw this extended reflection to a close by signaling some challenges faced by Christians in the Church, especially once they have recognized Jesus's invitation to join him at the twin tables of word and sacrament and find the course of their lives being reset accordingly. That is, when they have begun to escape today's software mindset and to discover that being Christian entails being Church. They are moving beyond the "earthly-minded," and learning what it means to give Christ their "full homage," in words from that ancient Eucharistic hymn, but this will likely involve certain challenges of Christian believing and belonging.

Christ our God to earth descending . . .

As flagged in the Introduction, many mainstream Christians in today's West struggle with the doctrinal content of Christian faith, while others take little notice of it. This is tied in with what the Church can and cannot mean to them. This is especially the case when Christ is not accorded the divinely exceptional status that a scriptural, credal, Eucharistic Church has traditionally proclaimed and celebrated. For instance, many non-Evangelical Anglicans do not recognize or acknowledge the fulness of God dwelling in Christ. Experience with lay education groups has shown me that Jesus Christ is not always acknowledged as savior and Lord. Some lay people do not feel a need for mercy and forgiveness, such that a lot of what Jesus brings is not deemed relevant. For Martha Tatarnic, reflecting on the same element of lay reluctance,

> A common reason for not believing in Jesus is it is too complicated. This is part of what I think people are getting at when they say that they are "spiritual, not religious." They believe in God, a higher power, perhaps a vague Creator. The specificity of Jesus, however, is a step too far. Likewise, my fellow parishioners can all mostly get on board with Jesus who is a great guy, inspiring teacher, even a healer and miracle worker. But in every study that I have ever led at any church, there is always a handful of people who want to leave it at that. They argue that in naming Jesus as God, we lose sight of the human being to whom we can actually relate, who invites us to follow in his footsteps, and who makes that invitation seem possible because Jesus is like us.[1]

Her final suggestion here—that a desire to follow Jesus may be compromised for people by claims for his divine status—is pastorally generous, and it may be true. Surely the approachability of Mary as a human figure, despite the official Roman Catholic dogma of her Bodily Assumption into heaven, is a major reason for her spiritual appeal in that church, providing a different face from the potentially stern and remote aspect of a divine Christ.

But if Tatarnic is right that this divine-human Christ proves off-putting to a common type of Anglican, I suspect that this might be a further example of software thinking. Jesus is allowed to represent God, but not to participate in God. Accordingly, Christians can become representatives of God, though without the risk of being drawn up into God's life, which is known as *theosis* and represents the mystical dimension of traditional Christianity. I suggest—and no doubt less generously in my assessments than Tatarnic—that to acknowledge Christ's traditional status according to Church doctrine is too much like hardware for some, and too disruptive of the software mentality that allows modern Christian individuals to remain comfortably in control of their own lives. This attitude maintains God and his Christ at a safe distance from secular priorities, to which an approachable, purely human Jesus provides the least potential disruption.

Much that fills out the realm of Christian belief will not take hold if those key Christological convictions are lacking. Yet so much commends itself once the central plank of incarnation is accepted. It can unlock the full panoply of Catholic doctrine, as classically argued by John Henry Newman in his *Grammar of Assent*, including the recognition that Christ is really, personally present in the Eucharistic bread and wine whereby he gives himself to us. If Church involvement is not Christ centered, however, then our engagement with the Church is unlikely to be meaningfully ecclesial. From this perspective, little or no sense will be made of the Church as a defining object and habitat of belief—one, holy, catholic, and apostolic. Nor can the Church aspire to be a nontribal tribe without the living reality of Christ at its heart.

Indeed, the perceived status of creeds for Christians is related to their assessments of the Church—of its importance or else its relative unimportance. Yet I would argue that moving beyond today's culturally mandated treatment of Church as software calls for a new appreciation of the credal contribution to maintaining Christian identity. The Apostles' and Nicene[2] creeds, which represent the formal reification of central gospel insights, occupy their liturgical roles (in baptism and Eucharist, respectively) as vehicles of Christian continuity and

comprehensiveness.[3] As decontextualized theological proposi-
tions met with in a mood of modern skepticism, however, the
credal articles can and often do prove distracting, irritating, or
perplexing—perhaps all three.

Those in liturgical churches who have these difficulties
may find it helpful to approach saying the creeds as something
like singing the national anthem, or as a venerable jazz theme
inviting creative new improvizations. As for the creeds' dogmatic content, their several articles are like balls kept in the air
as part of a never-ending dialogue in the Church. Theology
has always maintained this dialogue with its critical apparatus
fully deployed, so a range of answers is likely to be available for
interested questioners to pursue, debate, and make their own.
As with a national constitution and its perennially formative
role, we honour the creed best by responsibly receiving and
interpreting it in each new era and context.

. . . comes full homage to demand

Perhaps the ultimate sticking point is this: accepting institution, authority, and power in the Church as part of being
Christian is incompatible with today's high premium placed on
autonomy, and also its characteristic software mentality toward
everything religious. Yet the Church does make a claim on
Christians—unpopular perhaps, and intolerable for some, but
unavoidable. And the Church does not have to take a narrowly
sectarian form before it will press claims on us. The ordinary,
mainstream, liturgical Church has its own proper expectations
of its members. We humans are as institutional as we are com-
munitarian and linguistic after all, with institution, authority,
and power proving unavoidable in human history for good or
ill. But that is precisely why, in a world grown accustomed to
dysfunctional institutions, perverted authority, and abuses of
power, the Church's nontribal tribe must stake an alternative

claim on this same worldly ground. The earthly city is forever blessed and challenged by the heavenly city found integrally in its midst.

What is more, the gospel cannot but provide a constant impetus and challenge to churches in Christ's name. The Church must remain fully accountable. It is called to be a life-giving institution, Christlike in using the spiritual authority that he gives it through the Holy Spirit. Many have rightly criticized the Church in fidelity to its Lord for its failures in these respects. Prophets and reformers are sent by God to the Church. But it should not be forgotten that they also arise from the Church. And without love for the flawed Church that remains Christ's bride and body, prophets and reformers risk losing touch with Christ despite an earnest intent to serve him. This was Dietrich Bonhoeffer's warning. Likewise, today's progressives and activists pursuing their agendas through the Church are often a gift and a blessing from God, but their passion, if authentically Christian, will ultimately be for the Church's healing rather than for condemning and bypassing it.

James Alison gives witness in this regard as a leading advocate for the acceptance of gay and lesbian Christians within the Roman Catholic and wider Church. But his challenge to ecclesial homophobia is matched by his wry warning to gay and lesbian Catholics who have suffered at the Church's hands and end up hating the Church: that they had better get used to conservatives because there will be a lot of them in heaven. Here, the nontribal tribe shows its counter-cultural powers, so that tribalistic reactionaries are not matched in their self-defining rivalry by tribalistic progressives.

Sometimes the Church's faults as what Augustine called a *corpus permixtum* prove too much for people. There are many who have rightly needed to leave the Church, driven away by the disappointments, harms, traumas, and other psychological damage that it has caused them. We cannot expect that

all of these can be reconciled with the Church on this side of
heaven, though in the meantime they deserve patience, support, and a respectful hearing from the Church. Their path
toward psychological and spiritual healing may have justifi-
ably led them to alternative spiritual practices, or with relief
to lives of untroubled secularity—or perhaps to an alternative version of Church found online or in virtual reality, and
free of whatever drove them away from face-to-face church.
Such expedients should not be regarded harshly by Christians,
whose principled assessment of them, if authentic, must always
demonstrate pastoral generosity.

Countless others have been able to bear their disappointments with the Church and to stick with it. Clergy are well
represented in this group, along with many lay women and
Christians of same-sex orientation. Of clergy, it has been
quipped that if you get seasick, you should not seek a berth too
near the engine room. Martha Tatarnic knows the temptation
to leave in the face of hurts and frustrations inflicted by the
Church, and has also skated the edge of clergy burnout, but she
testifies to a countervailing impulse that makes it impossible
not to stay, sharing this hard-won hopefulness in her book *Why
Gather?* Many have faced the same temptations for various
reasons, but at such times, some words of Simon Peter to Jesus
in the Gospel may well come back to them: "Lord, to whom
can we go? You have the words of eternal life" (John 6:68).

One further option bears mention—a road less trav-
elled—involving the conscientious vocational decision to leave
one's established ecclesial home for a different Church. This
is often done in search of a hitherto missing fulness, as when
Anglo-Catholics "cross the Tiber" to become Roman Catholics, or when American Presbyterians, Methodists, or Baptists
join either the Episcopal Church or the Orthodox Church
of America. Such a step should only be taken with fear and
trembling, however, paying careful attention to Dietrich

Bonhoeffer's warning, in *Life Together*, that "He who loves his dream of a community more than the Christian community itself becomes a destroyer of the latter, even though his personal intentions may be ever so honest and earnest and sacrificial."[4] One can take comfort that Bonhoeffer's main concern was when visionary dreamers set about turning the Church into something new and "better"—a perennial temptation of reformers, zealots, and nuisances. However, sober ecclesial moves of this sort, undertaken from carefully considered motives and in a spirit of Christian charity toward one's former ecclesial home, are hopefully a different matter.

Given these various challenges of believing and belonging, it may be clearer why I address my question—Why Church—in the way that I have. Many try to argue for Church involvement in terms of benefits accruing to individual Christians. This is a useful consideration as far as it goes, but, let us be honest, it is a promise that can fail to deliver. And it leaves us on the receiving end of a consumerist exchange. I regard this widespread approach to be limited by a culturally conformist software mindset. Whereas Jesus's desire to share the Passover with us in the Eucharist, and to enlist us in the world-and-life-transforming Christian adventure through the Church, is more objective and more foundational. It promises to restore some of the hardware mentality that modern software Christianity has lost. It is an invitation to join him along with a whole forgiven, liberated humanity gathered around the Lord's table at peace—with God, with planet Earth, with each other, and with themselves. Why Church? To be part of that, to rejoice in that—Christianity as it was meant to be.

Notes

CHAPTER 1 Church as Hardware

1. See Augustine, *City of God.*

2. See Peter Brown, *Through the Eye of a Needle: Wealth, the Fall of Rome, and the Making of Christianity in the West, 350–550AD* (Princeton, NJ.: Princeton University Press, 2012), 80.

3. Stringer, *A Sociological History of Christian Worship*, 147.

4. Stringer, *A Sociological History of Christian Worship*, 139.

5. Stringer, *A Sociological History of Christian Worship*, 139–40.

6. Duffy, *The Stripping of the Altars.*

7. Haight, *The Christian Community in History*, Vol 2., *Comparative Ecclesiology*, 182.

8. Jenkins, *The Next Christendom*, i.

9. Hardy, *Beyond Belief*, xi.

10. Jenkins, *The Next Christendom*, 8; Kärkkäinen, *An Introduction to Ecclesiology*, 200.

11. Kärkkäinen, *An Introduction to Ecclesiology*, 201.

12. Jenkins, *The Next Christendom*, 99.

13. Jenkins, *The Next Christendom*, 10, 99, 250, 251.

14. Jenkins, *The Next Christendom*, 95.

15. Martin, "Pentecostalism: A Major Narrative of Modernity," in *On Secularization*, 141–154.

16. Jenkins, *The Next Christendom*, 97–98.

17. Jenkins, *The Next Christendom*, 125.

CHAPTER 2 Church as Software

1. Wuthnow, *After Heaven*, 3.

2. See Berger, *The Heretical Imperative.*

3. Taylor, *A Secular Age*, 38–39.

4. Taylor, *A Secular Age*, 192, 263.

5. Taylor, *A Secular Age*, 531.

6. Taylor, *A Secular Age*, 727.

7. Taylor, *A Secular Age*, 542.

8. Taylor, *A Secular Age*, 361, 676.

9. Kirkpatrick, *Community: A Trinity of Models*, 51.

10. Kirkpatrick, *Community: A Trinity of Models*, 52.

11. See Eagleton, *Culture and the Death of God*.

12. See Gillespie, *The Theological Origins of Modernity*.

13. For an excellent overview of this deep-seated opposition, its abandonment at Vatican II, and subsequent reactionary moves, see McGreevy, *Catholicism*.

14. Cavanaugh, *Migrations of the Holy*, 92.

15. Cavanaugh, *Migrations of the Holy*, 104.

16. Casanova, "Secularization, Enlightenment, and Modern Religion," in *Public Religions in the Modern World*, 11–39, at 19.

17. Healy, *Church, World and the Christian Life*, 98.

18. Lindbeck, "Ecumenical Imperatives for the 21st Century," 364.

19. Bruce, *God is Dead: Secularization in the West*, 86. For Bruce, today's utter deregulation of beliefs about God in the West means that God as we once knew him is now dead.

20. Williams, *Lost Icons*. See my *Abiding Faith*, 21.

21. Taylor, *A Secular Age*, 489.

22. Bellah, *Habits of the Heart*, 244.

23. de Lubac, *Catholicism*, 75–76.

24. Friedrich Schleiermacher, *The Christian Faith* (1830) (Edinburgh: T&T Clark, 1989), 103 (emphasis removed).

25. As argued by Stark and Finke, in *Acts of Faith*, 201.

26. Quoted in Delphine Norbellier, "German Protestants are shrinking in number," *La Croix*, 17 March 2023. Online at https://international.la-croix.com/news/religion/german-protestants-are-shrinking-in-number/17461 (accessed March 17, 2023).

27. Taylor, *A Secular Age*, 490–91.

28. See Brown, *The Death of Christian Britain*.

29. Badcock, *The House Where God Lives*, 335–36.

30. Healy, *Church, World and the Christian Life*, 16.

31. Bonhoeffer, *Life Together*, 17.

32. Bonhoeffer, *Sanctorum Communio*, 227.

33. Bonhoeffer, *Sanctorum Communio*, 227–28.

34. Stark and Finke, *Acts of Faith*, 200.

35. Taylor, *A Secular Age*, 519.

36. Bellah, *Habits of the Heart*, 48.

37. Taylor, *A Secular Age*, 289.
38. Wuthnow, *After Heaven*, 8 (emphasis added).
39. Haight, *The Christian Community in History*, Vol 2., *Comparative Ecclesiology*, 291.

CHAPTER 3 Abiding in the Vine

1. Bonhoeffer, *Sanctorum Communio*, 141.
2. Bonhoeffer, *Sanctorum Communio*, 128.
3. de Lubac, *Catholicism*, 63.
4. Kasper, *Theology & Church*, 156.
5. Bonhoeffer, *Sanctorum Communio*, 160–61.
6. Here I am indebted to John Zizioulas, *Being as Communion*, 18–122.
7. As argued by Jean-Luc Marion in *A Brief Apology for a Catholic Moment*.
8. Mission is commended as outward looking, but is it actually (and deceptively) invoked to help revitalize a flagging Church institution or else to justify centralizing and rationalizing measures? For the Church of England situation see Alison Milbank, *The Once and Future Parish*.
9. Brunner, *The Word and the World*, 108.
10. See Schmemann, *The World as Sacrament*.
11. Kasper, *Theology & Church*, 139.
12. Cavanaugh, *Migrations of the Holy*, 147.
13. Tomlin, *The Provocative Church*, 157.
14. Newbigin, *The Gospel in a Pluralist Society*, 227 (emphasis added).
15. Lohfink, *Does God Need the Church?*, 27.
16. Lohfink, *Does God Need the Church?*, 37.
17. Lohfink, *Does God Need the Church?*, 38.
18. See Halík, "The Afternoon of Christianity," 1.
19. Wuthnow, "From Dwelling to Seeking," in *After Heaven*, 1–18.
20. Halík, "The Afternoon of Christianity," 2.
21. See Macquarrie, "The Idea of a People of God," in *Theology, Church and Ministry*, 113–24.
22. Wuthnow, *After Heaven*, 5, 6.
23. Wuthnow, *After Heaven*, 16.
24. Timothy Noah, "How the GOP Lost its Brain" *The New Republic*, February 21, 2023. Online at https://newrepublic.com/article/170274

/gop-lost-brain?utm_source=newsletter&utm_medium=email&utm
_campaign=tnr_daily (accessed February 21, 2023).

25. I first introduced this concept of a nontribal tribe in the Conclusion of my book *René Girard and Secular Modernity*.

26. de Lubac, *Catholicism*, 53.

27. Pickard, *Seeking the Church*, 97 (emphasis removed).

28. See Gauchet, *The Disenchantment of the World*.

29. Lasch, *The Minimal Self*, 156. See also Fleming and Jane, *Modern Conspiracy*, arguing that conspiracy theories represent an attempt to reclaim human agency in the face of inscrutable yet inexorable wider forces.

30. For an unsparing exposé of MAGA-shaped American religiosity, see Jeff Sharlet, *Undertow: Scenes from a Slow Civil War*. For an analysis of the official and violent "othering" of American blacks along an extended historical arc, see Bellinger, *The Tree of Good and Evil*.

31. See Fisher, *The Chaos Machine*.

32. See Hopkins, "The Blessed Virgin compared to the Air we Breathe." See also my sermon contrasting the Blessed Virgin and a true *catholica* with social media's false *catholica*: "Identity and Connectedness: Mary in a Social Media Age" (prepared before I knew Hopkins's poem). A link is in the Bibliography.

CHAPTER 4 Treasures in Earthen Vessels

1. See the essay, "An Abusive Church Culture: Sexual Abuse and Systemic Dysfunction," in my *Church Matters*, 104–25.

2. GAFCON: The Global Anglican Futures Conference.

3. William Blake, "The Garden of Love." Online at https://www.poetry foundation.org/poems/45950/the-garden-of-love (accessed March 2, 2023).

4. The Gelasian Sacramentary, 5th century, from a translation by William Bright, 1861. Online at https://prayerandverse.com/2017/02/13 /that-wonderful-and-sacred-mystery/ (accessed March 2, 2023).

5. Hegstad, *The Real Church*, 115.

6. Healy, *Church, World and the Christian Life*, 26.

7. Healy, *Church, World and the Christian Life*, 37.

8. Berger, "Sociology and Ecclesiology," 70.

9. Healy, *Church, World and the Christian Life*, 37.

10. Tatarnic, *Why Gather?*, 80.
11. Augustine, *City of God*, XVIII.49, 831.
12. Augustine, *City of God*, XVIII.51, 833–35.
13. Williams, *Silence and Honey Cakes*, 92–93.
14. Article XIX, "Of the Church." "Modern History Sourcebook: The Thirty Nine Articles, 1571, 1662." Online at https://sourcebooks.fordham.edu/mod/1571-39articles.asp (accessed March 2, 2023).
15. A Pope's teaching can only be claimed as infallible "when, in the exercise of his office as shepherd and teacher of all Christians, in virtue of his supreme apostolic authority, he defines a doctrine concerning faith or morals to be held by the whole church." See *Decrees of the First Vatican Council*: "First Dogmatic Constitution on the church of Christ" (Session 4, July 18, 1870), Chapter 4.9. "On the infallible teaching authority of the Roman pontiff." In *Papal Encyclicals Online*, at https://www.papalencyclicals.net/councils/ecum20.htm (accessed March 2, 2023).
16. Küng, *The Church Maintained in Truth*, and especially the postscript to its English edition, "Why I Remain a Catholic," 75–87. He endorses the papal ministry, though not uncritically.
17. The Westminster Confession (1647), Chapter XXV.1. Online at https://reformed.org/historic-confessions/1647westminsterconfession/ (accessed March 30, 2023).
18. Hegstad, *The Real Church*, 2, 20.
19. Bonhoeffer, *Sanctorum Communio*, 280–81.
20. Kasper, "The Church as the Universal Sacrament of Salvation," in *Theology & Church*, 111–28, at 118.
21. Article XXVI, "Of the Unworthiness of the Ministers, which hinders not the effect of the Sacraments." "Modern History Sourcebook: The Thirty Nine Articles, 1571, 1662." Online at https://sourcebooks.fordham.edu/mod/1571-39articles.asp (accessed March 2, 2023).
22. See René Girard, *The Scapegoat*.
23. Bonhoeffer, *Life Together*, 17.
24. Bonhoeffer, *Sanctorum Communio*, 222.
25. Berger, "Sociology and Ecclesiology," 71–72
26. Radner, *Hope Among the Fragments*, 210–11.
27. Radner, *The End of the Church*, 352–53.

28. Bobrinskoy, *The Mystery of the Church*, 17.

29. Healy, *Church, World and the Christian Life*, 9.

30. Cavanaugh, *Migrations of the Holy*, 154–61, at 161.

31. See a translation of the Formula of Chalcedon online at http://www.grbc.net/wp-content/uploads/2015/09/The-Chalcedon-Confession.pdf (accessed March 3, 2023).

32. See John Webster, *Holiness*.

CHAPTER 5 Watermarks of the Church

1. Pickard, *Seeking the Church*, 128.

2. It is salutary to read the Augsburg Confession, noting its good will toward what went before. Online at https://bookofconcord.org/augsburg-confession/ (accessed March 17, 2023).

3. Küng, *The Church*, 268.

4. Moltmann, *The Church in the Power of the Spirit*, 341 (emphasis added).

5. See Haight, *Christian Community in History*, Vol. 2., *Comparative Ecclesiology*, Part I: "The Church in the Sixteenth Century," 13–288.

6. Lutheran pastors, like Anglican priests, could continue the Catholic practice of hearing confessions.

7. Dulles, *Models of the Church*, 125.

8. Haight, *Christian Community in History*, Vol. 2., *Comparative Ecclesiology*, 260.

9. Kärkkäinen, *An Introduction to Ecclesiology*, 71.

10. Moltmann, *The Church in the Power of the Spirit*, 339.

11. Moltmann, *The Church in the Power of the Spirit*, 340–41.

12. Kärkkäinen, *An Introduction to Ecclesiology*, 181–82.

13. Küng, *The Church*, 268.

14. Pickard, *Seeking the Church*, 131. Hans Küng once described the Church's sinfulness as following from that of the individual Christians within it (*The Church*, 323), which if true could likewise be regarded as an emergent property.

15. Absolute zero, thought to be the lowest possible temperature (i.e., when all matter freezes into crystalline solidity), is –273.15 degrees Celsius.

16. Hegstad, *The Real Church*, 229.

17. Küng, *The Church*, 273.

18. Kärkkäinen, *An Introduction to Ecclesiology*, 84.

19. Meszaros, "Yves Congar: The Birth of 'Catholic Ecumenism'," 6–7.

20. Pius XI, *Mortalium Animos*, Article 12. Online at https://www
.vatican.va/content/pius-xi/en/encyclicals/documents/hf_p-xi_enc
_19280106_mortalium-animos.html (accessed March 17, 2023).

21. Vatican II, "Decree on Ecumenism, *Unitatis Redintegratio*," III.13.

22. Dulles, *Models of the Church*, 126.

23. Vatican II, "Dogmatic Constitution on the Church, *Lumen Gentium*" (1964), I.8. Online at https://www.vatican.va/archive/hist_councils/ii
_vatican_council/documents/vat-ii_const_19641121_lumen-gentium
_en.html (accessed March 17, 2023).

24. Meszaros, "Yves Congar: The Birth of 'Catholic Ecumenism'," 19.

25. This is the 1888 Lambeth text; see online at https://www.anglican
communion.org/media/127722/1888.pdf. For the original 1886 Chicago statement, see online: https://www.anglicancommunion
.org/media/109011/Chicago-Lambeth-Quadrilateral.pdf. For an explanation of the process, see online: https://www.episcopalchurch
.org/glossary/chicago-lambeth-quadrilateral/ (all accessed March 30, 2023).

26. Küng, *The Church*, 282.

27. Küng, *The Church*, 275.

28. Küng, *The Church*, 285.

29. Kärkkäinen, *An Introduction to Ecclesiology*, 111.

30. Haight, *Christian Community in History*, Vol. 2., *Comparative Ecclesiology*, 422.

31. Vatican II, "Decree on Ecumenism, *Unitatis Redintegratio*," II.7.

32. Küng, *The Church*, 293.

33. These are the major contemporary ecumenical options set out by Haight, *Christian Community in History*, Vol. 2., *Comparative Ecclesiology*, 368. See also Tustin and Furberg (Co-Chairmen), "The Porvoo Common Statement," 1993.

34. Bobrinskoy, *The Mystery of the Church*, 237.

35. Pickard, *Seeking the Church*, 135.

36. Moltmann, *The Church in the Power of the Spirit*, 353.

37. Moltmann, *The Church in the Power of the Spirit*, 338.
38. Pickard, *Seeking the Church*, 138. I would say "declares itself" rather than "occurs" because of my previously mentioned concern that the marks are present rather than emergent.
39. Küng, *The Church*, 329.
40. Moltmann, *The Church in the Power of the Spirit*, 355.
41. Moltmann, *The Church in the Power of the Spirit*, 355.
42. Volf, *After Our Likeness*, 259–60, 262.
43. Pannenberg, *The Church*, 67.
44. Vatican II, "Decree on Ecumenism, *Unitatis Redintegratio*," I.3.
45. Pannenberg, *The Church*, 64.
46. Küng, *The Church*, 311.
47. Pickard, *Seeking the Church*, 142.
48. Zizioulas, *Being as Communion*, 158.
49. Moltmann, *The Church in the Power of the Spirit*, 349.
50. Moltmann, *The Church in the Power of the Spirit*, 352.
51. Volf, *After Our Likeness*, 267.
52. de Lubac, *Catholicism*, 49.
53. Moltmann, *The Church in the Power of the Spirit*, 338.
54. Küng, *The Church*, 312–13.
55. Küng, "Why I Remain a Catholic," in *The Church Maintained in Truth*, 75–87, at 85.
56. Generous Orthodoxy got its name from the Yale theologian Hans Frei; see Pulford, "Hans Frei: Beyond Liberal and Conservative."
57. Lindbeck, "Ecumenical Imperatives," 364.
58. Peterson, "Introduction," in *Generous Orthodoxies*, xvii–xxxiv, at xxi.
59. Hegstad, *The Real Church*, 21.
60. Küng, *The Church*, 351.
61. See Küng, *The Church*, 351.
62. Gaillardetz, *Ecclesiology for a Global Church*, 247.
63. Faith and Order Commission, The World Council of Churches, *Baptism, Eucharist and Ministry*, Ministry IV.B.35; c.f., Tustin and Furberg (Co-Chairmen), "The Porvoo Common Statement," IV.A.39.
64. Faith and Order Commission, The World Council of Churches, *Baptism, Eucharist and Ministry*, IV.A.34.

65. Moltmann, *The Church in the Power of the Spirit*, 359; c.f., Pannenberg, *The Church*, 68.

66. Shanks, *Anglicanism Reimagined*, 39. In an interesting variation, the Apostolic Restoration Movement within Pentecostalism seeks to revive the distinctive ministry of apostle, who is a figure of acknowledged supernatural power and spiritual authority. This development recovers something like a monarchical episcopate for an otherwise nonhierarchical tradition (yet some Pentecostal churches also have "bishops").

67. Faith and Order Commission, The World Council of Churches, *Baptism, Eucharist and Ministry*, Ministry IV.B.37, 38.

68. Faith and Order Commission, The World Council of Churches, *Baptism, Eucharist and Ministry*, Ministry VI.53.

69. Tustin and Furberg (Co-Chairmen), "The Porvoo Common Statement," I.B.8, IV.E.56, IV.C.49. From his Eastern Orthodox perspective, John Zizioulas also insists that episcopal succession entails a succession of communities—the Orthodox retain a much stronger bond between a bishop and a particular diocese than in the Western Church, with its typically more free-floating episcopal agents; see Zizioulas, *Being as Communion*, 198.

70. Tustin and Furberg (Co-Chairmen), "The Porvoo Common Statement," IV.D.53.

71. See their two websites: https://www.anglicancommunion.org /ecumenism/ecumenical-dialogues/roman-catholic/arcic.aspx, and https://iarccum.org (accessed March 23, 2023).

CHAPTER 6 Come and See

1. Bonhoeffer, *Sanctorum Communio*, 227.

2. Bonhoeffer, *Sanctorum Communio*, 282.

3. See James Alison, "Worship in a Violent World," in *Undergoing God*, 33–49.

4. Ferrone, "Earnest Desire," paragraph 2.

5. Pope Francis, *"Desiderio Desideravi,"* 10.

6. Pope Francis, *"Desiderio Desideravi,"* 17.

7. Pope Francis, *"Desiderio Desideravi,"* 27–65.

8. Halík, "The Afternoon of Christianity," 4.

9. Bobrinskoy, *The Mystery of the Church*, 155.

10. Moltmann, *The Church in the Power of the Spirit*, 355.

11. Tomlin, *The Provocative Church*, 161.

12. On Archbishop Justin Welby of Canterbury and his support for this initiative, which has emerged from the Evangelical powerhouse of Holy Trinity, Brompton, see Matthew Lasserre, "The man who's trying to halt the Church of England's decline," *La Croix*, March 21, 2023. Online at: https://international.la-croix.com/news/religion/the-man-whos-trying-to-halt-the-church-of-englands-decline/17485 (accessed March 21, 2023). For a sharply critical report on this, with searching analysis, see Alison Milbank, *The Once and Future Parish*.

13. I had been aware of a sort of "church" that someone started at a much earlier stage of these technological developments within the online game "Second Life." I was struck at the time by how the avatars chosen by "players" suggested a degree of mannered self-presentation, though of course this is not unknown in "real church" either.

14. See Carrette and King, *Selling Spirituality*.

15. See Cavanaugh, *Migrations of the Holy*.

Conclusion

1. Tatarnic, *Why Gather?*, 87.

2. Strictly speaking, this is the creed of Nicaea (from the year 325) as clarified and extended in the creed of Constantinople (381), with the rather later addition of a *filioque* clause (the Holy Spirit proceeding from the Father *and the Son*)—an innovation that was never accepted in the Christian East and is left out in some ecumenically-minded Western contexts today.

3. Texts of the Apostles' and Nicene Creeds can be found online at https://www.marquette.edu/faith/prayers-apostles.php, and at https://www.marquette.edu/faith/prayers-nicene.php (accessed August 31, 2023).

4. Bonhoeffer, *Life Together*, 17. It is reassuring that Bonhoeffer's words cited here come from his experience at the underground Finkenwalde Seminary of the Confessing Church, his having left the German Protestant mainstream—staying put is not the only faithful option.

Bibliography

Alison, James. *Undergoing God: Dispatches from the Scene of a Break-In* (New York and London: Continuum, 2006).

Augustine. *Concerning the City of God against the Pagans*, trans. Henry Bettenson (London: Penguin, 2003).

Badcock, Gary. *The House Where God Lives: Renewing the Doctrine of the Church for Today* (Grand Rapids, MI.: Eerdmans, 2009).

Bellah, Robert (et al). *Habits of the Heart: Individualism and Commitment in American Life*, 2nd edn. (Berkeley: University of California Press, 1996).

Bellinger, Charles K. *The Tree of Good and Evil: Or, Violence By the Law and Against the Law* (Eugene, OR.: Cascade, 2023).

Berger, Peter. *The Heretical Imperative: Contemporary Possibilities of Religious Affirmation* (New York: Doubleday, 1980).

―――. "Sociology and Ecclesiology," in Martin E. Marty, ed., *The Place of Bonhoeffer: Problems and Possibilities in His Thought* (London: SCM, 1963), 53–80.

Bobrinskoy, Boris. *The Mystery of the Church: A Course in Orthodox Dogmatic Theology*, trans. Michael Breck (Crestwood, NY.: St Vladimir's Seminary Press, 2012).

Bonhoeffer, Dietrich. *Life Together*, 5th edn. (1949), trans. John W. Doberstein (London: SCM, 1954).

―――. *Sanctorum Communio: A Theological Study of the Sociology of the Church* (1930), trans. Reinhard Kraus and Nancy Lukens, ed. Clifford J. Green (Dietrich Bonhoeffer's Works, Volume 1. Minneapolis: Fortress Press, 1998).

Brown, Callum G. *The Death of Christian Britain* (London: Routledge, 2001).

Bruce, Steve. *God is Dead: Secularization in the West* (Oxford: Blackwell, 2002).

Brunner, Emil. *The Word and the World* (London: SCM, 1931).

Carrette, Jeremy and Richard King. *Selling Spirituality: The Silent Takeover of Religion* (London: Routledge, 2004).

Casanova, José. *Public Religions in the Modern World* (Chicago: The University of Chicago Press, 1994).

Cavanaugh, William T. *Migrations of the Holy: God, State, and the Political Meaning of the Church* (Grand Rapids, MI.: Eerdmans, 2011).

Chesterton, G.K. *Where All Roads Lead*, in *Collected Works of G.K. Chesterton*, Volume 3. (1922) (San Francisco: Ignatius, 1990).

Cowdell, Scott. *Abiding Faith: Christianity Beyond Certainty, Anxiety, and Violence* (Eugene, OR.: Cascade, 2009).

———. *Church Matters: Essays and Addresses on Ecclesial Belonging* (Melbourne: Coventry, 2022).

———. "Identity and Connectedness: Mary in a Social Media Age." Online at https://stphilipsoconnor.org.au/discovery/sermons /docs/2019aug18_sc.php (accessed February 21, 2023).

———. *Is Jesus Unique? A Study of Recent Christology* (Theological Inquiries. Mahwah, NJ.: Paulist, 1996).

———. *René Girard and Secular Modernity: Christ, Culture, and Crisis* (Notre Dame, IN.: The University of Notre Dame Press, 2013).

de Lubac, Henri. *Catholicism: Christ and the Common Destiny of Man* (1947), trans. Lancelot C. Sheppard and Sister Elizabeth Englund, OCD (1950) (San Francisco: Ignatius, 1988).

Doyle, Dennis M. *Communion Ecclesiology: Visions and Versions* (Maryknoll, NY.: Orbis, 2000).

Duffy, Eamon. *The Stripping of the Altars: Traditional Religion in England 1400–1580* (New Haven, CT.: Yale University Press, 1992).

Dulles, Avery. *Models of the Church*, expanded edn. (New York: Doubleday Image, 1987).

Eagleton, Terry. *Culture and the Death of God* (New Haven, CT.: Yale University Press, 2014).

Elsberry, Terence L. *Leading With Love: Essentials of Church Leadership* (Eugene, OR.: Cascade, 2021).

Faith and Order Commission, The World Council of Churches. *Baptism, Eucharist and Ministry* (Faith and Order Paper 111. Geneva: The World Council of Churches, 1982).

Ferrone, Rita. "Earnest Desire: A new papal letter invites us to reflect on the liturgy," *Commonweal*, 27 August 2022. Online at https://

www.commonwealmagazine.org/earnest-desire (accessed March 28, 2023).

Fisher, Max. *The Chaos Machine: The Inside Story of How Social Media Rewired Our Minds and Our World* (New York: Little Brown, 2022).

Fleming, Chris and Emma A. Jane. *Modern Conspiracy: The Importance of Being Paranoid* (New York and London: Bloomsbury Academic, 2014).

Francis. "*Desiderio Desideravi*, On the Liturgical Formation of the People of God." Online at https://www.vatican.va/content/francesco /en/apost_letters/documents/20220629-lettera-ap-desiderio -desideravi.html (accessed March 28, 2023).

Gauchet, Marcel. *The Disenchantment of the World: A Political History of Religion*, trans. Oscar Burge (Princeton, NJ.: Princeton University Press, 1999).

Gillespie, Michael Allen. *The Theological Origins of Modernity* (Chicago: The University of Chicago Press, 2008).

Girard, René. *The Scapegoat*, trans. Yvonne Freccero (Baltimore, MD.: Johns Hopkins University Press, 1986).

Haight, Roger. *Christian Community in History*, Volume 2. *Comparative Ecclesiology* (New York: Continuum, 2005).

———. *Christian Community in History*, Volume 3. *Ecclesial Existence* (New York: Continuum, 2008).

Halík, Tomáš. "The Afternoon of Christianity: Church and Theology for a Post-Secular Age. A Templeton Colloquium at the NDIAS (November 15–17, 2015) by Msgr. Dr. Tomas Halik, 2014 Templeton Prize Laureate." Online at https://ndias.nd.edu /assets/181243/tomas_halik_colloquium_introductory_essay.pdf (accessed February 18, 2023). A fuller treatment is now available in English: see Tomáš Halík, *The Afternoon of Christianity: The Courage to Change*, trans. Gerald Turner (Notre Dame, IN.: The University of Notre Dame Press, 2024).

Hardy, Elle. *Beyond Belief: How Pentecostal Christianity is Taking Over the World* (London: Hurst, 2021).

Healy, Nicholas M. *Church, World and the Christian Life* (Cambridge: Cambridge University Press, 2000).

Hegstad, Harald. *The Real Church: An Ecclesiology of the Visible* (Church of Sweden Research Series 7. Eugene, OR.: Pickwick, 2013).

Hopkins, Gerard Manley. "The Blessed Virgin compared to the Air we Breathe." *Gerard Manley Hopkins Official Website*. Online at https://hopkinspoetry.com/poem/the-blessed-virgin/ (accessed February 21, 2023).

Jenkins, Philip. *The Next Christendom: The Coming of Global Christianity*, 3rd edn. (Oxford: Oxford University Press, 2011).

Kärkkäinen, Veli-Matti. *An Introduction to Ecclesiology: Ecumenical, Historical & Global Perspectives* (Downers Grove, IL.: IVP Academic, 2002).

Kasper, Walter. *Theology & Church*, trans. Margaret Kohl (London: SCM, 1989).

Kirkpatrick, Frank G. *Community: A Trinity of Models* (Washington, DC.: Georgetown University Press, 1986).

Küng, Hans. *The Church*, trans. Ray and Rosaleen Ockenden (New York: Sheed and Ward, 1967).

———. *The Church Maintained in Truth: A Theological Meditation*, trans. Edward Quinn (New York: Crossroad Seabury, 1980).

Lasch, Christopher. *The Minimal Self: Psychic Survival in Troubled Times* (New York: W.W. Norton, 1985).

Lindbeck, George. "Ecumenical Imperatives for the 21st Century," *Currents in Theology and Mission* 20 (1993), 360–74.

Lohfink, Gerhard. *Does God Need the Church? Toward a Theology of the People of God*, trans. Linda M. Maloney (Collegeville, MN.: Liturgical Press [Michael Glazier], 1999).

Macquarrie, John. *Theology, Church and Ministry* (New York: Crossroad, 1986).

Marion, Jean-Luc. *A Brief Apology for a Catholic Moment*, trans. Stephen E. Lewis (Chicago: University of Chicago Press, 2021).

Marr, Andrew. *Tools for Peace: The Spiritual Craft of St. Benedict and René Girard* (Lincoln, NE.: iUniverse, 2007).

McGreevy, John T. *Catholicism: A Global History from the French Revolution to Pope Francis* (New York: W.W. Norton, 2022).

Meszaros, Andrew. "Yves Congar: The Birth of 'Catholic Ecumenism'." In Paul Silas Peterson, ed. *Generous Orthodoxies*, 3–22.

Milbank, Alison. *The Once and Future Parish* (London: SCM, 2023).

Moltmann, Jürgen. *The Church in the Power of the Spirit: A Contribution to Messianic Ecclesiology*, trans. Margaret Kohl (New York: Harper & Row, 1977).

Newbigin, Lesslie. *The Gospel in a Pluralist Society* (Grand Rapids, MI: Eerdmans, 1989).

Newman, John Henry. *An Essay in Aid of a Grammar of Assent* (1870) (New York: Doubleday, 1955).

Pannenberg, Wolfhart. *The Church* (1977), trans. Keith Crim (Philadelphia: Westminster, 1983).

Peterson, Paul Silas, ed. *Generous Orthodoxies: Essays on the History and Future of Ecumenical Theology* (Eugene, OR.: Pickwick, 2020).

Pickard, Stephen. *Seeking the Church: An Introduction to Ecclesiology* (London: SCM, 2012).

Pulford, Ben. "Hans Frei: Beyond Liberal and Conservative," in Paul Silas Peterson, ed. *Generous Orthodoxies*, 99–117.

Radner, Ephraim. *The End of the Church: A Pneumatology of Christian Division in the West* (Grand Rapids, MI.: Eerdmans, 1998).

———. *Hope Among the Fragments: The Broken Church and Its Engagement of Scripture* (Grand Rapids, MI.: Brazos, 2004).

Schillebeeckx, Edward. *Christ the Sacrament of the Encounter with God*, trans. Paul Barrett (New York: Sheed and Ward, 1963).

———. *Church: The Human Story of God*, trans. John Bowden (New York: Crossroad, 1990).

———. *I Am a Happy Theologian: Conversations with Francesco Strazzari*, trans. John Bowden (New York: Crossroad, 1993).

Schmemann, Alexander. *The World as Sacrament* (London: Darton, Longman & Todd, 1974).

Shanks, Andrew. *Anglicanism Reimagined: An Honest Church* (London: SPCK, 2010).

Sharlet, Jeff. *Undertow: Scenes from a Slow Civil War* (New York: W.W. Norton, 2023).

Stark, Rodney. *The Rise of Christianity: How the Obscure, Marginal Jesus Movement Became the Dominant Religious Force in the Western World in a Few Centuries* (New York: HarperCollins, 1997).

Stark, Rodney and Roger Finke. *Acts of Faith: Explaining the Human Side of Religion* (Berkeley: University of California Press, 2000).

Stringer, Martin D. *A Sociological History of Christian Worship* (Cambridge: Cambridge University Press, 2005).

Tatarnic, Martha. *Why Gather? The Hope and Promise of the Church* (New York: Church Publishing, 2022).

Taylor, Charles. *A Secular Age* (Cambridge: MA.: The Belknap Press of Harvard University Press, 2007).

Tomlin, Graham. *The Provocative Church*, 4th edn. (London: SPCK, 2014).

Tustin, David and Tore Furberg (Co-Chairmen). "The Porvoo Common Statement," London, Council for Christian Unity of the General Synod of the Church of England, 1993. Online at https://porvoo communion.org/porvoo_communion/statement/the-statement -in-english/ (accessed March 9, 2023).

Vatican II. "Decree on Ecumenism, *Unitatis Redintegratio*" (1964). Online at https://www.vatican.va/archive/hist_councils/ii_vatican _council/documents/vat-ii_decree_19641121_unitatis-redintegratio _en.html (accessed March 9, 2023).

Volf, Miroslav. *After Our Likeness: The Church as the Image of the Trinity* (Grand Rapids, MI.: Eerdmans, 1998).

Webster, John. *Holiness* (London: SCM, 2003).

Williams, Rowan. *Lost Icons: Reflections on Cultural Bereavement* (Edinburgh: T&T Clark, 2000).

———. *Silence and Honey Cakes: The Wisdom of the Desert* (Oxford: Lion, 2003).

Wood, Susan. "Communion Ecclesiology: Source of Hope, Source of Controversy." *Pro Ecclesia* 2 no. 4 (1993), 424–32.

Wuthnow, Robert. *After Heaven: Spirituality in America Since the 1950s* (Berkeley, CA.: University of California Press, 1998).

Zizioulas, John. *Being and Communion: Studies in Personhood and the Church* (Crestwood, NY.: St Vladimir's Seminary Press, 1985).

Scripture Index

General Index